crochet

IN COLOR

TECHNIQUES AND DESIGNS
FOR playing with color

KATHY MERRICK

EDITOR **KATRINA LOVING**
DESIGNER **KARLA BAKER**
PHOTOGRAPHER **JOE HANCOCK**
PHOTO STYLIST **CAROL BEAVER**
TECHNICAL EDITORS **JULIE ARMSTRONG HOLETZ**
                   and **KAREN MANTHEY**
PRODUCTION **KATHERINE JACKSON**

Interweave Press LLC
201 East Fourth Street
Loveland, CO 80537-5655 USA
interweavestore.com

Printed in China by Asia Pacific Offset.

Library of Congress Cataloging-in-Publication
Data

Merrick, Kathy.
Crochet in color : techniques and designs for
playing with color / Kathy Merrick.
     p. cm.
Includes bibliographical references and index.
ISBN 978-1-59668-112-5 (pbk.)
1. Crocheting. 2. Crocheting--Patterns.
3. Color in art. I. Title.
TT825.M496 2009
746.43'4041--dc22

2009008961

10 9 8 7 6 5 4 3 2 1

DEDICATION

To Andrew Merrick and Charlotte Merrick, both spectacular human beings. And to John Merrick, for helping them turn out that way.

ACKNOWLEDGMENTS

Thanks to Liza Prior Lucy, Kaffe Fassett, Brandon Mably, and Maie, Taiu and Kersti Landra, Rhichard Devrieze, Kim Werker, Jane Brocket, Tricia Waddell, Tanis Gray, and Faith Hale, for letting me hang out with the cool kids.

Huge, important thanks to Katrina Loving, who patiently reads, fixes, understands, and then kindly explains how to create a good book.

Thanks also to Lisa Burke, Katherine Donner, Marie Duane, Franklin Habit, Selma Kaplan (my darling Axe Murderer), Annie Lawlor, The Fabulous Lucy Family: Drew, Big Al, and Little Bit, Ma, Barb Mahoney, Bill Moos and Mary Kay Lewis, Chris and Louann Moos, Carol Sulcoski, and Joe Wilcox, who give heartfelt opinions, companionship, and sorely needed advice. And make me laugh a lot.

And especially to my charming, hilarious, beloved niece Kathryn Lewis Moos, who always entertains me and makes me marvel: you're silly.

table *of contents*

introduction

I am a color junkie and a magpie.

Magpies are known for swooping down and capturing bits of tinfoil, food wrappers, and brightly colored pieces of string to add to their nests. This is very similar to the way I collect yarns. I often buy a skein or two of some beautiful yarn without necessarily knowing what I might use it for. I rarely buy enough of one yarn at a time for a specific purpose, but I often buy several colors of the same yarn. You see—I love color! I am excited by all the possibilities that lie within such an assortment of pretty colors.

I think the magpie approach of collecting bits and pieces of whatever catches your eye is wonderful for getting rid of the fear of putting colors together in a crochet project. Unfortunately, using many colors together in one project is something that intimidates many crocheters.

My extensive experience with crochet patterns has revealed that there is a niche that needs to be filled. I have seen many projects that are fascinating and take much technical skill, but even those of us who consider ourselves "arty" or fashionable may be hard-pressed to wear the finished pieces outside the house. There are also many projects that are practical and usable but not very challenging or exciting to make.

My hope is that you will find this book a helpful resource that merges the best of both worlds. You will find projects with exciting forays into color combined with challenging yet accessible patterns. There are tips for choosing and combining colors as well as examples that will encourage you to just let go and have fun playing with color combinations. Soon you will see that color is exciting, not intimidating, and you'll be surprised at how easy it is to crochet colorful, attractive, and useful treasures.

— kathy

7

exploring COLOR

I know that there are crocheters who don't yelp with joy at the sight of a yarn store wall or a webpage loaded with yarn in a plethora of colors. The idea of trusting yourself enough to choose colors with which to create an entire sweater, blanket, or shawl can be scary.

The best way to ease yourself into working with color is to start with a small-scale project. You will learn about what appeals to you and what looks attractive as you work on it. You might begin by copying a pleasing color scheme from a beautiful postcard, a magazine photo, a piece of printed fabric (look at the selvedges for a color key), or a book illustration.

When you've decided on your color inspiration, look for materials that are sold in small individual quantities. Your local craft store stocks hundreds of colors of embroidery floss and crewel yarn, which come in eight or ten yards in each skein. The best thing about this method is that you can add many colors, shades, and tones without having to invest in whole skeins of yarn in colors that may not work out.

Now that you've collected a lively handful of colors, make a simple piece, such as a scarf worked lengthwise in half-double crochet or a hat worked in the round. You want to be free to try out your color scheme without concentrating too much on shaping or clever stitch patterns.

Another great experiment is using colors chosen at random to learn how different colors look next to each other. Start by going back to the embroidery floss display and picking out twenty or so colors that catch your eye. Put them into a bag or basket and make a ball from them, taking each one out without really thinking about it. By the time you start crocheting, you'll have forgotten the order in which you wound up the colors and the changes will be a surprise.

You may find you love how silvery shades look next to yellows or how much variety you can find by using a number of pale washed-out pastels.

Finally, try choosing some colors you don't really like and then add or subtract until you get something that looks beautiful. Vibrant combinations of pinks and oranges may be overwhelming, but add a little gray and a little dull green and it looks smoother. The quiet stone colors of a northern beach may look dull and insipid, but shots of periwinkle and chartreuse make them sparkle.

The most important point to remember here is simply this: experiment with color and have fun doing it! The projects in the following pages will ease you gently into using color and then carry you along as you become more and more confident in your color-work abilities. And for those of you who are ready for a challenge right away—never fear, there are plenty of projects employing more advanced techniques and fearless color combinations.

one or two COLORS

Often yarn comes in a color that just jumps out and begs you to make something exciting with it. It may be a particularly lovely shade of your favorite color or an outrageous color you don't often choose, such as chartreuse or bright orange. Using just one or two colors gives you an opportunity to make interesting details, fancy stitches, and intricate shaping to complement the simplicity of your color palette. The most important thing is just to have fun—you might be surprised at how quickly you fall in love with color and find yourself itching to add a few more to your designs.

PLEATED *hat*

finished size

21" (53.5 cm) circumference; 6" (15 cm) long after sewing.

yarn

DK weight (#3 Light) in pink multi.

SHOWN: Sheep Shop Yarn, Sheep Three (70% merino wool, 30% silk; 325 yd [297 m]/3.5 oz [100 g]): #G43 spring, 1 skein.

hook

G/7 (4.5 mm) or size needed to obtain gauge.

notions

Tapestry needle; split-ring marker.

gauge

18 sts x 14 rows = 4" (10 cm) in hdc worked in the round through back loops only.

I have spent a lot of time in Milan. It's an exciting, vibrant city, full of galleries and beautiful shops. On an old winding street called Via Santa Marta is Trattoria Milanese, a favorite restaurant where, in June, you can watch guys taking cherries off of branches for your dessert while they listen to the World Cup on the radio. Via Santa Marta also houses a tiny clothing shop full of handmade garments and accessories made with intriguing combinations of knitting, crochet, and sewing. When I happened upon the delicately colored soft wool used in this project, all of those memories from Milan came together. The result was this hat with sewn pleats and cherry-colored dashes.

....

» Entire hat is worked through back loops only.

» Do not join rounds with slip stitch. Instead work in a spiral, continuing around and marking the first stitch of each round as you go.

pleated hat

Ch 3, pm in first ch from hook (counts as first hdc), 7 hdc in 3rd ch from hook, do not join—8 hdc.

RND 1: 2 hdc through blo in marked ch, 2 hdc-blo in each st around—16 sts.

RND 2: *2 hdc blo in next st, hdc-blo in next st; rep from * around—24 sts.

RND 3: *2 hdc blo in next st, hdc-blo in next 2 sts; rep from * around—32 sts.

RND 4: *2 hdc blo in next st, hdc-blo in next 3 sts; rep from * around—40 sts.

RNDS 5–12: Working in established patt, cont inc each rnd by 8 sts until there are 11 hdc between each inc—104 sts.

RND 13: Hdc blo in each st around.

FINISH FIRST RIDGE

RND 14: *Hdc2tog, hdc in next 11 sts; rep from * around—96 sts.

RND 15: *Hdc2tog, hdc in next 10 sts; rep from * around—88 sts.

RNDS 16–18: Hdc-blo in each st around.

WORK SECOND RIDGE

RND 19: *2 hdc into next st, hdc in next 10 sts; rep from * around—96 sts.

RND 20: *2 hdc into next st, hdc in next 11 sts; rep from * around—104 sts.

RNDS 21–22: Rep Rnds 14 and 15—88 sts.

RNDS 23–27: Hdc blo in each st around. Fasten off.

FINISHING

Turn hat inside out. With tapestry needle and one strand of yarn, make two pleats by sewing together the loops from Rnd 10 and the loops from Rnd 14 using herringbone stitch (p. 116); sew together the loops of Rnd 20 and the loops of Rnd 24 using herringbone stitch.

Turn hat right side out, count 20 sts from center back and then sew the next 6 sts of each pleat together on right side of hat with herringbone stitch. Weave in loose ends.

FIREFLY *cardigan*

finished size

S (M, L, XL) fits 33 (38, 43, 48)" (84 [96.5, 109, 122] cm) bust circumference. Sweater shown is size S.

yarn

Laceweight (#0 Lace) in green-yellow

SHOWN: Lorna's Laces, Helen's Lace (50% wool, 50% silk; 1250 yd [1125 m]/4 oz [113 g]): #54 firefly, 3 (3, 3, 4) skeins.

hook

F/5 (3.75 mm) or size needed to obtain gauge.

notions

Tapestry needle; straight pins; seven $^3/_8$" (2 cm) round buttons.

gauge

20 sts x 16 rows = 4" (10 cm) in hdc.

An unusual color is enough to make a flattering shape stand out. When I saw this green-yellow laceweight wool/silk yarn in a store in Philadelphia, I thought all it needed was some interesting shaping to make a pretty cardigan. It is tightly gathered at the waist in one spot on the back and each side of the front with nicely shaped armholes and a slight puff on the sleeves. A narrow lace pattern fills the edging and collar, and only half-double crochet is needed to work the body.

notes

» Yarn is held doubled throughout.

» Beginning chain counts as a stitch.

» Work armhole and sleeve increases and decreases two stitches in from edge.

» Decreases are worked as hdc2tog.

special stitches

V-STITCH (V-ST):

(Dc, ch 1, dc) in st or sp indicated.

V-STITCH PATTERN (V-ST PATT):

ROW 1: Skip 4 ch (counts as 1 dc, skip 1 ch), *v-st in next ch, skip 2 ch; rep from * across, ending row with skip 1 ch, dc in last ch, turn.

ROW 2: Ch 3 (counts as first dc here and throughout), *v-st in same ch as v-st from previous row; rep from * across, ending with dc in tch of prev row, turn.

ROW 3: Ch 3, *v-st in ch-1 of v-st from 2 rows below; rep from * across, ending with dc in tch of prev row, turn.

ROW 4: Ch 3, dc in tch 2 rows below, *v-st in ch-1 of v-st from 2 rows below, v-st in between v-sts from 2 rows below; rep from * across, ending with dc in tch of prev row, turn.

ROW 5: Ch 3, *v-st in ch-1 of v-st from prev row; rep from * across, ending with dc in tch of prev row, turn.

ROW 6: Ch 3, *v-st in ch-1 of v-st from prev row; rep from * across, ending with dc in tch of prev row, turn.

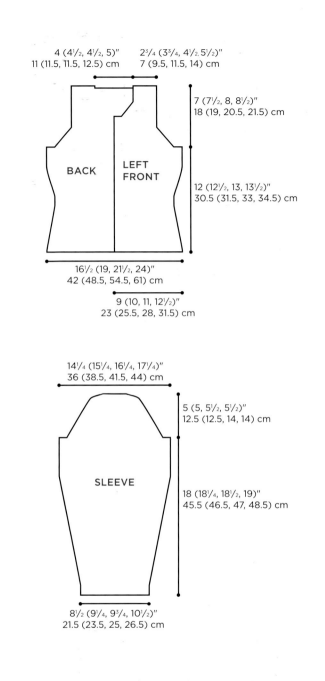

4 (4½, 4½, 5)"
11 (11.5, 11.5, 12.5) cm

2¾ (3¾, 4½, 5½)"
7 (9.5, 11.5, 14) cm

7 (7½, 8, 8½)"
18 (19, 20.5, 21.5) cm

BACK

LEFT FRONT

12 (12½, 13, 13½)"
30.5 (31.5, 33, 34.5) cm

16½ (19, 21½, 24)"
42 (48.5, 54.5, 61) cm

9 (10, 11, 12½)"
23 (25.5, 28, 31.5) cm

14¼ (15¼, 16¼, 17¼)"
36 (38.5, 41.5, 44) cm

5 (5, 5½, 5½)"
12.5 (12.5, 14, 14) cm

SLEEVE

18 (18¼, 18½, 19)"
45.5 (46.5, 47, 48.5) cm

8½ (9¼, 9¾, 10½)"
21.5 (23.5, 25, 26.5) cm

firefly cardigan

BACK

With yarn held doubled, ch 87 (99, 111, 123). Work Rows 1–3 of v-st patt for border—27 (31, 35, 39) v-sts.

NEXT ROW (RS): Ch 2 (counts as hdc here and throughout), work 1 hdc in each dc and ch-sp across, do not work st in tch, turn—82 (94, 106, 118) hdc. Work even in hdc until back measures 6 (6¼, 6¾, 7¼)" (15 [16, 17, 18.5] cm) from bottom edge ending with a RS row.

BEGIN PEPLUM SHAPING

ROW 1 (WS): Ch 2, hdc in next 30 (36, 42, 48) hdc, [hdc2tog] 10 times, hdc across to end, turn—72 (84, 96, 108) hdc.

ROW 2: Work 1 row even.

ROW 3: Ch 2, hdc in next 30 (36, 42, 48) hdc, [hdc2tog] 5 times, hdc across to end—67 (79, 91, 103) hdc.

Work 4 rows even.

BEGIN SHAPING TO ACCOMMODATE BUST

NEXT ROW (RS): Ch 2, hdc in next 27 (33, 39, 45) hdc, [2 hdc in next hdc] 5 times, hdc into next hdc, [2 hdc in next hdc] 5 times, hdc across to end, turn—77 (89, 101, 113) hdc.

Work even until back measures 12 (12½, 13, 13½)" (30.5 [31.5, 33, 34.5] cm).

BEGIN ARMHOLE SHAPING

ROW 1: Sl st over 6 (6, 7, 7) sts, ch 1, hdc across to last 6 (6, 7, 7) sts, turn leaving rem sts unworked—65 (77, 87, 99) hdc.

ROW 2: Ch 2, hdc in next hdc, [hdc2tog] twice, hdc across to last 6 sts, [hdc2tog] twice, hdc in last 2 sts, turn—61 (73, 83, 95) hdc.

Work 2 decs at each end of every other row 2 more times—53 (65, 75, 87) hdc. Work 1 row even. Work 1 dec at each end of next row, then every 4th row 1 (1, 2, 2) times—49 (61, 69, 81) hdc.

Work even until armhole measures 7 (7½, 8, 8½)", (18 [19, 20.5, 21.5] cm) ending with a WS row.

BEGIN SHOULDER SHAPING (RS)

Work 14 (19, 23, 28) hdc for right shoulder. Fasten off. Skip next 21 (23, 23, 25) hdc, join yarn in next st, work 14 (19, 23, 28) hdc for left shoulder. Fasten off.

RIGHT FRONT

With yarn held doubled, ch 48 (54, 60, 66). Work Rows 1–3 of v-st patt for border—14 (16, 18 20) v-sts.

NEXT ROW (RS): Ch 2, work 1 hdc in each dc and ch-sp across, do not work st in tch, turn—43 (49, 55, 61) sts. Work even in hdc until back measures 6 (6¼, 6¾, 7¼)" (15 [16, 17, 18.5] cm) from bottom edge ending with a RS row.

BEGIN PEPLUM SHAPING

ROW 1 (WS): Ch 2, hdc in next 11 (14, 17, 20) hdc, [hdc2tog] 5 times, hdc in next 21 (24, 27, 30) hdc, turn—38 (44, 50, 56) hdc.

ROW 2: Work 1 row even.

ROW 3: Ch 2, hdc in next 11 (14, 17, 20) hdc, [hdc2tog] 2 times, hdc in next 22 (25, 28, 31) sts, turn—36 (42, 48, 54) hdc.

Work 4 rows even.

BEGIN BUST SHAPING

NEXT ROW (RS): Ch 2, hdc in next 19 (22, 25, 28) hdc, [2 hdc in next hdc] 4 times, hdc across to end, turn—40 (46, 52, 58) hdc.

Work even until front measures 12 (12½, 13, 13½)" (30.5 [31.5, 33, 34.5] cm) ending with a RS row.

BEGIN ARMHOLE SHAPING

ROW 1 (WS): Sl st over 6 (6, 7, 7) sts, ch 1, hdc across, turn—34 (40, 45, 51) hdc.

ROW 2: Ch 2, hdc across until 6 sts remain, [hdc2tog] twice, hdc in last 2 hdc, turn—32 (38, 43, 49) hdc.

Rep Row 2 of armhole shaping every other row 2 times more, turn—28 (34, 39, 45) hdc.

Work 1 row even. Work 1 dec at armhole edge of next row, then every 4th row 1 (1, 2, 2) times—26 (32, 36, 42) hdc. Work even until piece measures 3½ (4, 4½, 5)" (9 [10, 11.5, 12.5] cm) from beginning of armhole ending with a RS row.

BEGIN NECK SHAPING

Work even across until 10 (11, 12, 13) sts remain, hdc2tog, hdc in next 2 hdc, turn leaving rem sts unworked—19 (25, 29, 35) hdc. Work 1 dec at neck edge of every other row 4 (4, 5, 5) more times—15 (21, 24, 30) hdc.

Work even until front length matches back length. Fasten off.

LEFT FRONT

Work as for Right Front, reversing shaping.

SLEEVES (MAKE 2)

Ch 48 (51, 54, 57).

BEGIN CUFF: Work 6 rows of v-st patt for border.

NEXT ROW (RS): Ch 2, work 1 hdc in each dc and ch-sp across, do not work st in tch, turn—43 (46, 49, 52) hdc. Work even in hdc for 6 (6, 7, 7) rows.

NEXT ROW (INC ROW): Ch 2, hdc in first hdc, 2 hdc in next hdc, work across to last 4 sts, 2 hdc in next hdc, hdc in last 2 hdc—45 (48, 51, 54) hdc. Continue in hdc working inc row every 4th row 13 (14, 15, 16) times—71 (76, 81, 86) hdc. Work even until sleeve measures 17 (17 1/4, 17 1/2, 18)″ (43 [44, 44.5, 45.5] cm) from cuff.

BEGIN SHAPING ARMHOLE

Sl st over 7 (7, 8, 8) sts, ch 2, hdc across to last 6 (6, 7, 7) sts, turn leaving rem sts unworked—59 (64, 67, 72) hdc.

NEXT ROW (DEC ROW): Ch 2, hdc in next hdc, [hdc2tog] twice, hdc across to last 6 sts, [hdc2tog] twice, hdc in last 2 hdc—55 (60, 63, 68) hdc. Continue in hdc working dec row every other row 8 (8, 9, 9) times—23 (28, 27, 32) hdc.

NEXT ROW: Ch 2, hdc in next hdc, [hdc2tog] 9 (12, 12, 14) times, hdc in last 3 (2, 1, 2) hdc. Work 1 row even. Fasten off.

LEFT FRONT BORDER

Beginning at neck, work 64 (67, 70, 73) hdc down to bottom of piece, turn. Work Rows 1–3 of v-st patt—19 (20, 21, 22) v-sts. Fasten off.

RIGHT FRONT BORDER

Work as for Left Front Border except begin at bottom of piece and work to neck.

With RS together, sew Back to Right and Left Fronts at shoulders, using mattress stitch (p. 117).

COLLAR

With RS facing, join yarn to upper Right Front Border, work 6 hdc evenly across row ends of border, hdc around neckline, working 1 hdc for each st and 1 hdc for each row end, ending with 6 hdc across left front border, turn—72 (78, 84, 90) sts. Work 6 rows of v-st patt, working 2 v-sts into each space—144 (156, 168, 180) sts. Fasten off.

FINISHING

Weave in loose ends. With RS together, pin sleeve cap into armhole, matching sleeve and side seams and gathering cap at the top center of sleeve at shoulder seam.

Sew sleeve and side seams, using mattress stitch.

Using spaces between v-sts on right front border for a buttonhole guide, sew 7 (7, 8, 8) buttons evenly spaced to left front band, beginning at top of neckline and ending just above bottom border. For buttonholes, use ch-sps between v-sts on Right Front Border corresponding to buttons.

Gently steam block (p. 118) garment to achieve a smooth and even appearance.

DOUBLE BOBBLE *scarf*

finished size

58" (147.5 cm) long x 7" (18 cm) wide, including bobble edge.

yarn

Worsted weight (#4 Medium) in magenta.

SHOWN: Cascade Yarns, Luna (100% Peruvian Tanguis cotton; 82 yd [74 m]/1.75 oz [50 g]): #711 magenta, 2 skeins.

hook

J/10 (6 mm) or size needed to obtain gauge.

notions

Stitch markers (pm); tapestry needle.

gauge

12 sts x 8 rnds= 4" (10 cm) alternating rows of dc and hdc.

Years ago I made a scarf with a deep ruffle surrounding an oblong of double crochet. When wrapped twice around the neck it reminded me of the sort of ruffs seen in portraits of Queen Elizabeth I. Two rounds of bobbles on chains in a very rich color of slightly crinkly cotton give a similar yet softer effect. Fold the scarf in half lengthwise, put it around your neck from back to front, and pull the ends through the loop—pretty!

stitch guide

BOBBLE: Work 4 hdc in 2nd ch from hook; remove
hook from loop, insert hook from front to back in
1st hdc; pull loop through first hdc.

double bobble scarf

Refer to the stitch diagram at right for
assistance.

Ch 154.

RND 1: Skip first 3 ch (counts as first dc), 2 dc in
4th ch from hook, 2 dc in next ch, dc in each ch
to 2nd to last ch, 2 dc in next ch, 3 dc in last ch,
pm in first dc, rotate piece and begin working in
free lps of foundation ch, 2 dc in next ch, dc in
each ch across to last ch, 2 dc in last ch, sl st in
first dc to join—308 dc.

RND 2: Ch 2 (counts as first hdc), hdc in same
dc, 3 hdc in next dc, 2 hdc in next dc, hdc in
each dc across to pm, 2 hdc in marked dc, 3 hdc
in next dc, move pm to first dc, 2 hdc in next dc,
hdc in each dc across, sl st in 2nd ch of beg ch-2
to join—316 hdc.

RND 3: Ch 3 (counts as first dc), dc in next hdc,
2 dc in next hdc, 3 dc in next hdc, 2 in next hdc,
dc in each hdc across to pm, 2 dc in marked hdc,
3 dc in next hdc, 2 dc in next hdc, dc in each hdc
across, sl st in first dc to join—324 dc.

RND 4: Ch 4 (counts as first dc and ch 1), skip
next dc, *(dc in next dc, ch 1, skip next dc) across
to 3-dc group*, [dc, ch 1] twice in each dc of
3-dc group, skip next dc; rep from * once, rep
from * to * across, sl st in first dc to join—170 ch-1
sps.

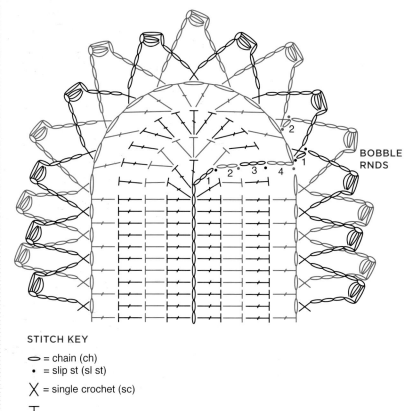

BOBBLE RNDS

STITCH KEY

⬯ = chain (ch)

• = slip st (sl st)

✕ = single crochet (sc)

T = half double crochet (hdc)

† = double crochet (dc)

⬮ = bobble

BOBBLE RND 1: Sl st into first ch-sp, ch 1, sc in
same sp, *ch 5, work bobble, ch 4, skip next ch-
sp, sc into next ch-sp; rep from * around, sl st in
first sc of rnd—85 bobbles.

BOBBLE RND 2: Sl st across into first skipped
ch-sp, and working behind previous Bobble Rnd,
ch 1, sc in same ch-sp, *ch 6, work bobble, ch 5,
sc into next skipped ch-sp; rep from * around, sl
st in first sc of rnd—85 bobbles.

Fasten off.

FINISHING

Weave in loose ends. Handwash in cool water
and block (p. 118) to finished measurements.

GRANADA *shawl*

finished size

40" (101.5 cm) at longest point x 70"
(178 cm) at widest point.

yarn

DK weight (#3 light) in orange; fingering
weight (#1 super fine) in light blue-gray.

SHOWN: Rowan Kidsilk Haze (70% super
kid mohair, 30% silk; 229 yd [210 m]/.9 oz
[25 g]): #596 marmalade (MC) 2 balls.

Rowan 4-ply Soft (100% merino wool;
191 yd [175 m]/1.75 oz [50 g]): #387 rain
cloud (CC) 1 ball.

hook

G/6 (4 mm) or size needed to obtain
gauge

notions

Tapestry needle.

gauge

Each motif measures 10" (25.4 cm)
diagonally across square from corner to
corner.

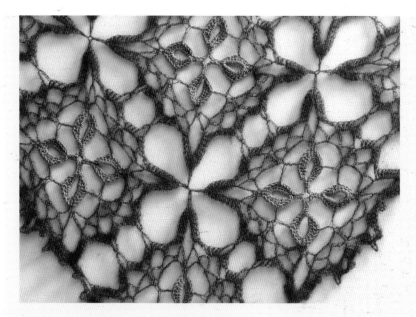

I have admired the motif featured in this shawl for quite some
time. When viewed from a short distance, it's reminiscent of the
Moorish filigree work that can be seen in southern Spain and in
the city of Granada. I realized it would be very effective worked in
two contrasting yarns in two contrasting colors. It's lightweight,
dramatic, and not really complicated to work up.

If you choose different yarns, keep the center yarn somewhat
dense and the outside yarn filmy so you don't lose the stark effect.

» When joining in MC, leave a 4″ (10 cm) tail, and work the first few sts with working yarn and tail together.

» Shawl begins with one full motif and subsequent motifs are joined on the last round as you work.

» It's easier to make the Half Motifs when the Full Motifs are finished.

shawl

See stitch diagram on p. 31 for assistance.

FIRST FULL MOTIF

RND 1: With CC, *ch 16, sl st in 13th ch from hook, turn, (sc, hdc, 14 dc, hdc, sc) into loop just made, sc in each of 3 rem ch; rep from * 3 times, sl st in tail end of first loop, being careful not to twist—4 loops made. Fasten off CC.

RND 2: Join MC with sl st in 8th dc of one loop, ch 1, sc in same st, *ch 9, skip 3 dc, tr2tog in next dc and 3rd dc of next loop, ch 9, skip 3 dc, sc in next 2 dc; rep from * 3 times, omitting final sc, sl st in first sc.

RND 3: Ch 1, sc in first sc, *[ch 5, sc] 3 times into next ch-9 sp, [sc, ch 5] 3 times into next ch-9 sp, sc in next 2 sc; rep from * 3 times, omitting final sc, sl st in first sc—24 ch-sps.

RND 4: Ch 1, 2 sl st into next ch-5 sp, ch 1, sc into same sp, *[ch 6, sc into next ch-5 sp] twice, sc into next ch-5 sp, [ch 6, sc into next ch-5 sp] twice, ch 9, sc into next 5-ch sp; rep from * 3 times, omitting final sc, sl st in first sc.

RND 5: Ch 1, 2 sl st into first ch-6 sp, ch 1, sc into same sp, *[(4 dc, ch 4, 4 dc) into next ch-6 sp] twice, sc into next ch-6 sp, (9 dc, ch 4, 9 dc) into next ch-9 sp, sc into next ch-6 sp; rep from * 3 times, omitting final sc, sl st in first sc.

SUBSEQUENT FULL MOTIFS

Work as for First Motif through Rnd 4.

RND 5: Ch 1, 2 sl st into first ch-6 sp, ch 1, sc into same sp, [(4 dc, ch 2, sl st into corresponding ch-4 sp of prev motif, ch 2, 4 dc) into next ch-6 sp] twice, sc into next ch-6 sp, (9 dc, ch 2, sl st into corresponding ch-4 sp of prev motif, ch 2, 9 dc) into next ch-9 sp, finish rnd as for First Motif, ending with (9 dc, ch 2, sl st into corresponding ch-4 sp of prev motif, ch 2, 9 dc) in last ch-9 sp, sl st in first sc.

Continue making and joining motifs following construction diagram below, begin with First Motif as Row 1, then join 2 motifs for Row 2. Continue adding 1 motif on every row, until there are 6 rows, with 6 motifs in top row (Row 6).

HALF MOTIFS

ROW 1: With CC, *ch 12, dc in 4th ch from hook, 2 dc in each of next 3 ch, hdc in next ch, sc in each ch to end (one point made)*, ch 16, sl st in 13th ch from hook to make a loop, turn, (sc, hdc, 14 dc, hdc, sc) into loop, sc in remaining 3 ch, rep from * to *, sl st in last sc of beginning arm. Fasten off CC.

ROW 2: With MC, sl st in top of ch-3 at end of first point, ch 1, sc in top of ch-3, sc in next dc, ch 9, skip 3 dc, work tr2tog in next dc and 3rd dc of next loop, ch 9, skip 3 dc, sc in next 2 dc, ch 9, skip 3 dc, tr2tog in next dc and 5th dc from end of last point, twisting last arm of first row so sts face loop, ch 9, sc in last 2 dc, turn.

ROW 3: Ch 1, sc in first 2 sc, *[ch 5, sc] 3 times into next ch-9 sp, [sc, ch 5] 3 times into next ch-9 sp, sc in next 2 sc; rep from * once, turn.

ROW 4: Ch 1, sc in each of first 2 sc, 2 sl st into next ch-sp, ch 1, sc into same sp, *[ch 6, sc into next ch-5 sp] twice, sc into next ch-sp, [ch 6, sc into next ch-sp] twice*, ch 9, sc into next ch-sp, rep from * to * once, 2 sl st in same ch-sp as last sc worked, sc in each of last 2 sc, turn.

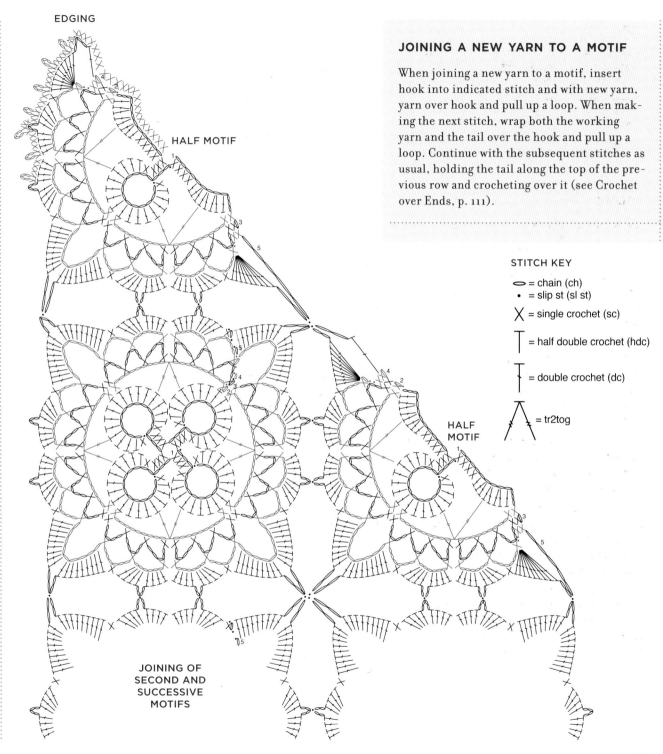

EDGING

HALF MOTIF

HALF MOTIF

JOINING OF
SECOND AND
SUCCESSIVE
MOTIFS

JOINING A NEW YARN TO A MOTIF

When joining a new yarn to a motif, insert hook into indicated stitch and with new yarn, yarn over hook and pull up a loop. When making the next stitch, wrap both the working yarn and the tail over the hook and pull up a loop. Continue with the subsequent stitches as usual, holding the tail along the top of the previous row and crocheting over it (see Crochet over Ends, p. 111).

STITCH KEY

∾ = chain (ch)

• = slip st (sl st)

✕ = single crochet (sc)

⊤ = half double crochet (hdc)

╪ = double crochet (dc)

⋀ = tr2tog

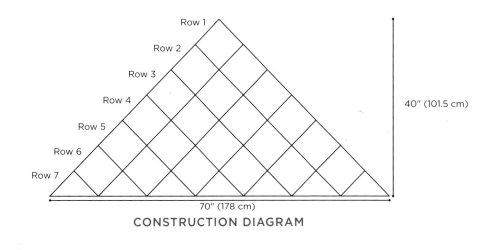

Row 1
Row 2
Row 3
Row 4
Row 5
Row 6
Row 7

40" (101.5 cm)

70" (178 cm)

CONSTRUCTION DIAGRAM

FIRST AND LAST HALF MOTIF

ROW 5: Ch 5 (counts as first dc, ch 2), sl st into corresponding ch-4 of prev row of motifs, ch 2, 9 dc into next sc, sc into next ch-sp, [(4 dc, ch 2, sl st into corresponding ch-4 sp of prev row of motifs, ch 2, 4 dc) into next ch-6 sp] twice, sc into next sp, (9 dc, ch 2, sl st into corresponding ch-4 sp of prev row, ch 2, 9 dc) into next ch-9 sp, sc into next sp, [(4 dc, ch 4, 4 dc) into next ch-6 sp] twice, sc into next ch-6 sp, 9 dc in next sc, ch 4, dc in last sc. Fasten off.

HALF MOTIFS JOINED ON BOTH SIDES

ROW 5: Ch 5 (counts as first dc, ch 2), sl st into corresponding ch-4 of prev row of motifs, ch 2, 9 dc into next sc, sc into next ch-sp, [(4 dc, ch 2, sl st into corresponding ch-4 sp of prev row of motifs, ch 2, 4 dc) into next ch-6 sp] twice, sc into next sp, (9 dc, ch 2, sl st into corresponding ch-4 sp of prev row, ch 2, 9 dc) into next ch-9 sp, sc into next sp, [(4 dc, ch 2, sl st into corresponding ch-sp of prev row, ch 2, 4 dc) into next ch-6 sp] twice, sc into next ch-6 sp, 9 dc in next sc, ch 2, sl st into corresponding ch-sp of prev row, ch 2, dc in last sc. Fasten off.

Make 7 Half Motifs, joining them to prev row of motifs as you go.

FINISHING

EDGING: With point of shawl at bottom, join MC with sl st to ch-sp at upper left Half Motif, sc in same sp, *(sc, ch 4, sc) in next dc, sc in each of next 3 dc; rep from * down left side, then up right side, treating each dc as 1 st and each ch-sp as 4 sts for repeat. Continue working sc only, evenly across top of shawl.

Weave in loose ends.

Wet block (p. 118) shawl to finished measurements.

STRIPES

The simplest way to be adventurous with color is to make stripes.

Try taking a large number of warm or cool colors and stagger them in panels to make a dynamic but fairly easy blanket or shawl. Or try selecting a number of related or even unrelated colors of variegated yarns and work them in wide stripes to eliminate the worry of pooling and stacking. Use a limited palette and an organized stripe pattern and then rely on odd numbers to change the expected pattern (see an example of this in the Butterfly Turtleneck on p. 45).

TROPICAL *stripe wrap*

finished size

95″ (241 cm) long x 48″ (122 cm) wide, after blocking.

yarn

Fingering weight (#1 Super Fine) in green/yellow, turquoise/black/fuchsia, turquoise/black/fuchsia/orange/yellow, brown/raspberry, red/burgundy, chartreuse rainbow, orange rainbow, green/brown, deep green/blue rainbow, orange, and brown/red/green stipple.

SHOWN: Koigu KPPM (100% premium merino wool; 175 yd [157 m]/ 1.75 oz [50 g]): #P822 (D [green/yellow]), 2 skeins; #P139 (A [turquoise/black/fuchsia]); #P326 (B [turquoise/black/fuchsia/orange/yellow]); #P324 (C [brown/raspberry]); #P860 (E [red/burgundy]); #P135 (F [chartreuse rainbow]); #P133a (G [orange rainbow]); #P504 (H [green/brown]); #P823 (I [deep green/blue rainbow]); #P627 (J [orange]); #P711 (K [brown/red/green stipple]), 1 skein each.

hook

G/6 (4 mm) or size needed to obtain gauge.

notions

Tapestry needle.

gauge

17 sts x 16 rows = 4″ (10 cm) in hdc.

This cozy wrap is all about a striking group of colors—the colors themselves inspired the creation. Look for several colors of equal intensity for this project. Place a group of colors that attract you in a row and then pull out any that stand out as too pale or too dark.

Bright yellows, greens, and oranges are featured here, but turquoise, sea greens, and blues would be beautiful, as would periwinkle, chartreuse, leaf green, and magenta. The one-sided edge featured on the wrap adds a little softness without becoming too sweet.

tropical stripe wrap

With A, ch 402.

ROW 1: Hdc in 3rd ch from hook and in each ch across, turn—400 hdc.

ROW 2: Ch 2, hdc in first hdc and in each hdc across, turn.

Rep Row 2 until A is used up. Change to B and use it up, then C, D (1 skein will be used), E, F, G, H, I, and D (2nd skein will be used). Change to J and work 5 rows. Fasten off.

BORDER

Refer to the stitch diagram at right for a reduced sample of the border.

ROW 1: With K, beginning at bottom left edge, ch 3 (counts as first dc here and throughout), dc in first ch, dc in each ch across, turn—401 dc.

ROW 2: Ch 3, dc in first dc, skip next dc, dc in next dc, skip next dc, *3 dc in next dc, skip next dc, dc in next dc, skip next dc; rep from * across, ending with 2 dc in last dc, turn—401 dc.

ROW 3: Ch 3, skip next dc, *(2 dc, ch 3, sl st in 1st ch of ch-3, dc) all in next dc, ch 1, skip 3 dc; rep from * across to last st, dc in last dc, turn.

ROW 4: Ch 1, sc in first dc, *ch 6, sc into next ch-1 sp; rep from * across, ending with ch-6, sc in last dc. Fasten off; weave in loose ends.

FINISHING

To block, machine wash in cold water on gentle cycle. Tumble dry on low heat until not quite dry.

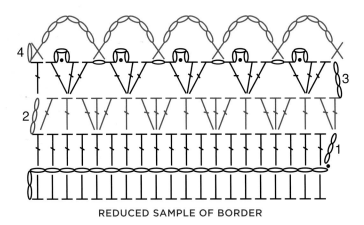

REDUCED SAMPLE OF BORDER

STITCH KEY

⬯ = chain (ch)
• = slip st (sl st)
✕ = single crochet (sc)
⊤ = half double crochet (hdc)
⊤ = double crochet (dc)
= picot

WARM COLORS
striped blanket

finished size

47" (119.5 cm) wide x 62" (157.5 cm) long, after blocking.

yarn

Worsted weight (# 4 Medium) in muted orange, deep magenta, brown, fuchsia, yellow-green, muted red/beige, deep pink, burgundy, deep orange, beige, muted green-brown, light purple, dark pink-red, bright purple-pink, pale yellow, pale beige/red, rust, pale orange, medium pink, and beige/brown.

SHOWN: Malabrigo Merino Worsted (100% merino wool: 215 yd [190 m]/3.5 oz [100 g]): #123 rhodesian (A); #44 geranio (B); #161 rich chocolate (C); #93 fuchsia (D); #35 frank ochre (E); #79 red java (F); #21 cactus flower (G); #41 burgundy (H); #94 bergamota (I); #70 beige (J); #181 marron oscuro (K); #193 jacinto (L); #102 sealing wax (M); #184 shocking pink (N); #19 pollen (O); #194 cinnabar (P); #16 glazed carrot (Q); #72 apricot (R); #39 molly (S); # 50 roanoke (T), 1 skein each.

hook

I/9 (5.5 mm) or size needed to obtain gauge.

notions

Smooth flat worsted-weight wool yarn for sewing (the Malabrigo yarn is too loosely spun for sewing); tapestry needle.

gauge

14 sts x 11 rows= 4" (10 cm) in hdc.

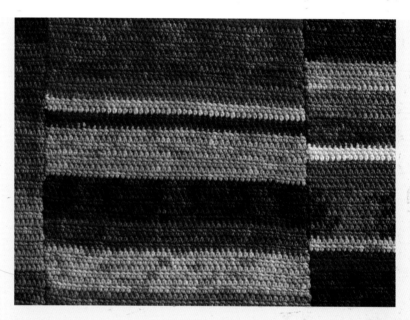

This blanket is the greedy result of seeing a wall full of warm reds, pinks, oranges, and yellows in soft Malabrigo yarn and listening to Astor Piazzola play a tango. It is made in three panels sewn together with borders sewn around the panels. The strong color contrasts give the blanket lots of movement, something like that tango.

notes

» Turning chains do not count as stitches.

» The body of the blanket is made of three panels, following the Color Guide for each panel.

» Follow Panel instructions on p. 43 for each of the three panels.

» Borders are worked in rectangles, following the Stripe Guide on p. 43.

CONSTRUCTION DIAGRAM

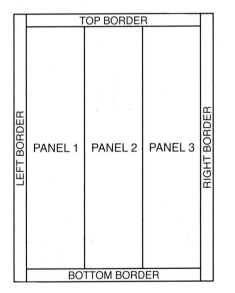

color guide

PANEL 1: 2 rows O, 3 rows K, 4 rows G, 6 rows R, 3 rows A, 1 row I, 6 rows H, 3 rows E, 4 rows N, 2 rows F, 2 rows J, 3 rows Q, 2 rows L, 6 rows A, 2 rows D, 1 row C, 2 rows G, 2 rows O, 4 rows S, 3 rows E, 5 rows M, 2 rows P, 1 row D, 2 rows L, 3 rows R, 4 rows B, 3 rows A, 6 rows N, 2 rows K, 1 row J, 1 row O, 4 rows B, 3 rows H, 2 rows Q, 1 row F, 3 rows C, 1 row E, 2 rows G, 4 rows J, 5 rows D, 3 rows F, 1 row E, 1 row O, 3 rows A, 3 rows Q, 2 rows N, 6 rows T, 2 rows L, 2 rows K, 2 rows M, 4 rows S, 1 row C, 3 rows I, 1 row G, 2 rows R.

PANEL 2: 5 rows A, 1 row L, 6 rows H, 3 rows M, 2 rows R, 7 rows C, 4 rows Q, 2 rows O, 2 rows B, 2 rows A, 4 rows G, 1 row J, 3 rows E, 7 rows K, 2 rows M, 3 rows I, 3 rows C, 1 row N, 5 rows R, 1 row O, 1 row G, 1 row H, 4 rows A, 2 rows J, 5 rows F, 5 rows E, 3 rows D, 7 rows T, 2 rows I, 3 rows R, 1 row L, 4 rows Q, 3 rows S, 4 rows K, 2 rows O, 6 rows M, 1 row E, 4 rows J, 3 rows H, 3 rows B, 3 rows P, 2 rows C, 3 rows A, 1 row D, 4 rows F, 7 rows I, 1 row L, 1 row O, 2 rows Q.

PANEL 3: 3 rows S, 4 rows C, 1 row D, 1 row E, 1 row P, 3 rows A, 5 rows G, 2 rows F, 3 rows I, 3 rows J, 1 row K, 2 rows L, 5 rows A, 2 rows M, 3 rows N, 2 rows O, 4 rows F, 1 row R, 2 rows D, 1 row C, 1 row Q, 5 rows P, 3 rows H, 2 rows E, 6 rows B, 3 rows A, 1 row J, 1 row L, 2 rows N, 1 row T, 3 rows K, 4 rows M, 2 rows P, 2 rows D, 3 rows G, 2 rows O, 3 rows R, 2 rows I, 5 rows T, 2 rows E, 3 rows B, 4 rows J, 1 row S, 1 row A, 3 rows H, 4 rows P, 2 rows Q, 1 row O, 3 rows G, 2 rows C, 3 rows F, 2 rows L, 1 row R, 1 row K, 5 rows A, 2 rows I, 3 rows N, 3 rows T, 1 row E, 2 rows J, 2 rows G, 1 row M.

stripe guide

TOP BORDER Stripe Sequence: S, A, Q, K, B, F, O, P, T, I, J, D.

BOTTOM BORDER Stripe Sequence: A, P, C, G, T, E, Q, H, M, R, N, A.

LEFT BORDER Stripe Sequence: L, C, E, G, A, H, S, R, T, P, B, K, Q, J, M, C.

RIGHT BORDER Stripe Sequence: K, M, B, O, Q, J, N, A, P, F, T, E, G, H, I, R.

striped blanket

PANEL (MAKE 3 ACCORDING TO THE COLOR GUIDES AT LEFT)

Ch 52.

ROW 1: Work hdc into 3rd ch from hook, hdc in each ch to end, turn—50 hdc.

ROW 2: Ch 2, work hdc in each hdc across, turn.

Rep Row 2 throughout panel, changing colors as directed in the Color Guide at left.

Following the construction diagram at left, with sewing yarn and tapestry needle, use mattress stitch (p. 117) to sew Panel 1 to Panel 2, then sew Panel 3 to the other edge of Panel 2.

BORDER

Ch 12.

ROW 1: Work hdc in 3rd ch from hook, hdc in each ch to end, turn—10 hdc.

ROW 2: Ch 2, hdc in each hdc across, turn.

Rep Row 2 throughout, working each color for 10 rows, following the Stripe Guide above.

FINISHING

Sew top and bottom borders to each short end of the blanket using mattress stitch and then Sew the left and right Borders to each long side.

Gently steam block (p. 118) blanket to finished measurements.

BUTTERFLY *turtleneck*

finished size

S (M, L, XL) fits 32 (35½, 39, 42½)" (81 [90, 99, 108] cm) bust circumference. 21 (21½ , 22, 22½)" (53.5 [54.5, 56, 57] cm) long from highest point of shoulder to bottom. Sweater shown is size S.

yarn

Fingering weight (#1 Super Fine) in gold, blue, green, brown, orange, and light purple.

SHOWN: Crystal Palace, Panda Silk (52% bamboo, 43% superwash merino wool, 5% combed silk; 204 yd [188 m]/1.75 oz [50 g]): #3002 butterscotch (A); #3001 pearl blue (B); #3005 bamboo green (C); #3021 café mocha (D); #3004 orange zest (E); #3020 lilac mist (F), 2 skeins each for all sizes.

hook

D/3 (3.25 mm) or size needed to obtain gauge.

notions

Tapestry needle for sewing.

gauge

22½ sts and 20 rows = 4" (10 cm) in hdc.

I love stripes of all sorts—awning stripes, men's striped shirts, beach umbrellas, flags—all are appealing sources for translation into crocheted garments. You only need a good assortment of yarn to choose from. This beautiful bamboo/wool/silk yarn with its subtle sheen comes in many great colors. I chose some pastels reminiscent of Renoir paintings and simply staggered the narrow and wide stripes. They became a perfect foil for the butterfly stitch border.

» Beginning ch-2 does not count as a stitch.

» Decreases for neck shaping should be worked three stitches in from neck edge. If neck edge is at the beginning of the row, work one stitch, then work decrease over next two stitches. If neck edge falls at the end of a row, work across until three stitches remain, work decrease over next two stitches, then work final stitch.

special stitch:

BUTTERFLY STITCH PATTERN (BUTTERFLY ST PATT)

(Multiple of 11)

ROW 1 (WS): Ch 2, hdc in first 3 hdc, *ch 5, skip 5 hdc, hdc in next 6 hdc; rep from * across, ending with hdc in last 3 hdc, turn.

ROW 2: Ch 2, hdc in first 3 hdc, *ch5, skip ch-5 sp, hdc in next 6 hdc; rep from * across, ending with hdc in last 3 hdc, turn.

ROW 3: Rep Row 2.

ROW 4 (RS): Ch 2, hdc in first 3 hdc *ch 2, hdc around ch of prev 3 rows, ch 2, hdc in next 6 hdc; rep from * across, ending hdc in last 3 hdc, turn.

Rep Rows 1–4 for patt.

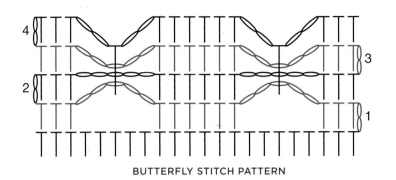

BUTTERFLY STITCH PATTERN

STITCH KEY

⬯ = chain (ch)

T = half double crochet (hdc)

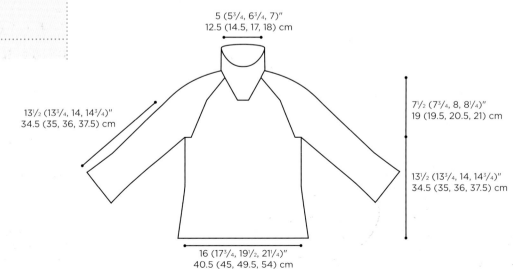

5 (5³/₄, 6³/₄, 7)"
12.5 (14.5, 17, 18) cm

13¹/₂ (13³/₄, 14, 14³/₄)"
34.5 (35, 36, 37.5) cm

7¹/₂ (7³/₄, 8, 8¹/₄)"
19 (19.5, 20.5, 21) cm

13¹/₂ (13³/₄, 14, 14³/₄)"
34.5 (35, 36, 37.5) cm

16 (17³/₄, 19¹/₂, 21¹/₄)"
40.5 (45, 49.5, 54) cm

stripe guide

STRIPE SEQUENCE FOR BODY: 6 rows A, 1 row D, 6 rows B, 1 row E, 6 rows C, 1 row F, 6 rows D, 1 row A, 6 rows E, 1 row B, 6 rows F, 1 row C.

butterfly turtleneck

BACK

With A, ch 101 (112, 123, 134). Hdc in 3rd ch from hook, hdc in each ch across; turn—99 (110, 121, 132) hdc.

Work 4 rows each in butterfly st patt in the foll color order: A, B, C, D, E, and F—9 (10, 11, 12) ch-sps.

BEGIN BODY

With A, ch 2, *hdc in each hdc to ch-2 sp, 2 hdc in ch-2 sp, skip next hdc, 2 hdc in next ch-2 sp; rep from * across, ending hdc in last 3 hdc, turn—90 (100, 110, 120) hdc. Work even in hdc following Stripe Sequence for Body (according to the Stripe Guide above) until Back measures 13 1/2 (13 3/4, 14 1/4, 14 3/4)" (34.5 [35, 36, 37.5] cm) long from bottom edge and ending with a WS row. Fasten off.

BEGIN RAGLAN SHAPING

ROW 1: With RS facing and continuing in Stripe Sequence for Body, attach yarn to 8th (9th, 10th, 11th) st from right edge, ch 2, hdc in same st and in each st across until 7 (8, 9, 10) hdc remain, turn, leaving rem sts unworked—76 (84, 92, 100).

ROW 2: Ch 2, hdc in first 2 hdc, hdc2tog, hdc in each hdc across until 4 hdc remain, hdc2tog, hdc in last 2 hdc, turn—74 (82, 90, 98) hdc.

ROW 3: Work 1 row even.

Rep last 2 rows 11 (12, 13, 14) times—52 (58, 64, 70) hdc. Rep Row two 12 (13, 14, 15) times—28 (32, 36, 40) hdc. Fasten off.

FRONT

Work as for Back until you have 56 (62, 70, 76) sts, about 4 (4¼, 4½, 4¾)" (10 [11, 11.5, 12] cm) from beg of raglan shaping.

BEGIN NECK SHAPING

NEXT ROW: Continue raglan shaping and at the same time begin neck shaping, work hdc over first 22 (27, 32, 37) hdc, turn, leaving rem sts unworked.

Continue raglan shaping and at the same time dec at neck edge every other row 7 (7, 8, 8) times. Continue raglan shaping until Front length matches Back. Fasten off.

Join yarn, 22 (27, 32, 37) sts in from opposite edge of row where neck shaping began. Work other side of neck to match, reversing shaping. Fasten off.

SLEEVES (MAKE 2)

With A, ch 57 (61, 68, 72).

ROW 1: Hdc in 3rd ch from hook and each ch across, turn—55 (59, 66, 70) hdc.

ROW 2: Ch 2, hdc in next 3 (5, 3, 5) hdc, *ch 5, skip 5 hdc, hdc in next 6 hdc; rep from * across ending with ch-5, skip 5 hdc, hdc in last 3 (5, 3, 5) hdc, turn—5 (5, 6, 6) ch-sps.

Work Rows 2–4 of butterfly st patt with A, then work 4 rows each of butterfly st patt in B, C, D, E, and F.

NEXT ROW: With A, ch 2, *hdc in each hdc to ch-2 sp, 2 hdc in ch-2 sp, skip next hdc, 2 hdc in next ch-2 sp; rep from * across, ending hdc in last 3 (5, 3, 5) hdc, turn—50 (54, 60, 64) hdc. Work in hdc following Stripe Sequence for Body and increasing 1 st at beg and end of every other row 9 (10, 10, 11) times, then every 4th row 4 (4, 5, 5) times—76 (82, 90, 96) hdc. Work even, if necessary, until sleeve measures 13½ (13¾, 14¼, 14¾)" (34.5 [35, 36, 37.5] cm) from beginning.

BEGIN RAGLAN SHAPING

Keeping to Stripe Sequence for Body, attach yarn to 8th (9th, 10th, 11th) st, ch 2, hdc in same st and in each st across until 7 (8, 9, 10) hdc remain, turn—62 (66, 72, 76) hdc.

ROW 2: Ch 2, hdc in first hdc, hdc2tog, hdc in each hdc across until 3 hdc remain, hdc2tog, hdc in last hdc, turn—60 (64, 70, 74) hdc.

ROW 3: Work 1 row even.

Rep last 2 rows 6 (7, 9, 10) more times, then Row two 22 (23, 22, 23) times—4 (4, 8, 8) hdc. Work even, if necessary, until sleeve armhole length matches body armhole length. Fasten off.

FINISHING

With WS facing, line up front of sleeve armholes to front panel armholes, then sew together using mattress stitch (p. 117). Sew back right sleeve armhole to back right armhole, using mattress stitch.

COLLAR

With RS facing, join A at back left neck edge, ch 2, hdc around neck edge working 1 hdc for each st and 1 hdc for each row end, turn. Work 4 rows of butterfly st patt with A, then in each of B, C, D, and E. Fasten off.

Sew back left to back left sleeve, with WS facing continuing up neck edge.

Sew sleeves and side seams, with WS facing using mattress stitch.

Handwash, then lay flat to dry.

color BLOCKS

Working in blocks of color can be as straightforward as choosing three or four cheerful colors and making large motifs into a wrap. Or crocheting large swaths of quieter variegated color in a very simple lace pattern. Two contrasting motifs together can set up a great framework for a big throw; you can have a lot of fun adding bright colors to a neutral background. The wonderful thing about color blocks is that you can work a variety of shades into pattern work without losing the actual pattern. This chapter will offer you an opportunity to continue adding colors to your crochet in a very straightforward way.

CHAIN LACE *big fat scarf*

finished size

72" (183 cm) long x 16" (41 cm) wide.

yarn

Fingering weight (# 1 Super Fine) in pale magenta, gold/green, light red, pastel rainbow, green, brick red, deep blue, yellow/orange, and dusty pink/blue.

SHOWN: Koigu Painters Palette Premium Merino (KPPM) (100% merino wool: 175 yd [160 m]/1.75 oz [50 g]): #P713 (A [pale magenta]); #P509 (B [gold/green]); #P339 (C [light red]); #P118L (D [pastel rainbow]); #P719 (E [green]); #P610 (F [brick red]); #P706D (G [deep blue]); #P707 (H [yellow/orange]); #P714 (I [dusty pink/blue]), 1 skein each.

hook

F/5 (3.75 mm) or size needed to obtain gauge.

notions

Tapestry needle.

gauge

2 pattern repeats x 14 rows = 4" (10 cm).

General wisdom says that variegated yarns don't make lace or fancy stitch patterns stand out enough to be seen. In this case, however, there was something magical about the combination of an easy lace pattern and these "stippled" colors that really worked. Although the colors of each skein differ quite a bit, from yellow to red to blue, they are all medium tones and none jumps out more boldly than another. That's what makes this work—keeping the colors to the same intensity allows the lace pattern to really shine through.

notes

» Turning chains do not count as stitches.

» Work with each skein until it is used up. For the last block, work about four rows to make sure you'll have enough yarn to end with a complete row.

» Lace is generally wet-blocked to stretch and show off the lace, but here the interesting texture of the Chain Lace occurs by simply steaming the piece, if necessary.

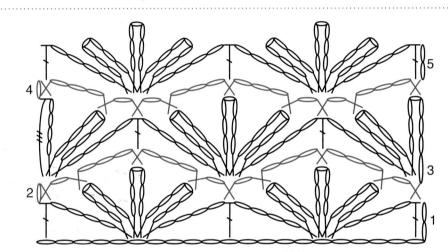

REDUCED SAMPLE OF PATTERN

STITCH KEY

⬯ = chain (ch)

X = single crochet (sc)

T = double crochet (dc)

T = double treble crochet (dtr)

scarf

See stitch diagram on p. 54 for a sample of the patt.

Ch 363 (multiple of 10+3).

ROW 1: Dc in 3rd ch from hook, *skip 4 ch, ch 4, [sc, ch 7] 3 times in next ch, sc in same ch, skip 4 ch, ch 4, dc in next ch; rep from * across, turn—36 patt reps.

ROW 2: Ch 1, *sc in dc, ch 1, [sc in next ch-7 loop, ch 3] twice, sc in next ch-7 loop, ch 1; rep from *across, ending with sc in last dc, turn.

ROW 3: Ch 8, (sc, ch 7, sc) in first sc, *skip (ch 1, sc, ch 3), ch 4, dc in next sc, skip (ch 3, sc, ch 1), ch 4, [sc, ch 7] 3 times in next sc, sc in same sc; rep from * across, ending with (sc, ch 7, sc, ch 4, dtr) in last sc, turn.

ROW 4: Ch 1, sc in ch-4 loop, ch 3, sc in next ch-7 loop, *ch 1, sc in next dc, ch 1, [sc in next ch-7 loop, ch 3] twice, sc in next ch-7 loop; rep from * across, ending with ch 3, sc into last ch-8 loop, turn.

ROW 5: Ch 2, dc in first sc, *skip (ch 3, sc, ch 1), ch 4, [sc, ch 7] 3 times in next sc, sc in same sc, skip (ch 1, sc, ch 3), ch 4, dc in next sc; rep from * across, turn.

Rep Rows 2–5 using A, B, C, D, E, F, G, and H until end of each skein. End with Row 2 or Row 4, then work 4 rows using I.

Fasten off. Weave in ends.

FINISHING

Steam block (p. 118) the finished piece gently to smooth and shape.

BLOCKS *coat*

finished sizes

S (M, L, XL) fits 37 (40½, 44, 48)" (94 [103, 112, 122] cm) bust circumference. Coat shown is size S.

yarn

Worsted weight (#4 Medium) in orange/red heather, light gray heather, dark teal/purple heather, olive heather, aqua/green heather, yellow/black heather, light yellow/beige heather, black/white heather, garnet, and light brown/gray heather.

SHOWN: Cascade Yarns, Cascade 220 Wool (100% wool; 220 yd [200 m]/3.5 oz [100 g]): #2425 (A; orange/red heather); #8400 (B; light gray heather); #9336 (C; dark teal/purple heather), #9448 (D; olive heather); #9451 turquoise (E; aqua/ green heather); #9459 (F; yellow/black heather); #9460 (G; light yellow/beige heather); #4002 (H; black/white heather); #9341 (I; garnet); #4011 light brown/gray heather (J), 1 skein each.

hook

J/10 (6 mm) or size needed to obtain gauge.

notions

8 (9, 9, 10) ¾" (2 cm) square buttons, tapestry needle for sewing up; sewing needle and sewing thread (or tapestry needle and yarn) for attaching buttons.

gauge

13 sts x 12 rows = 4" (10 cm).

I was looking out my window at a Pennsylvania October when I started thinking about this cozy project. When autumn comes, I like the idea of a big comfy jacket in strong colors, with the added bonus of nice big pockets. The wonderful thing about this coat is that you could easily use a different color combination—say, sky blue, cream, rose, lavender, and aqua—to welcome spring. This is an easy introduction to working crochet intarsia because the blocks are simple and regular. Master the easy color changes here and then move on to circles or stars.

notes

» Entire garment is worked in half double crochet.

» Turning chain does not count as a stitch.

» Intarsia is a colorwork technique in which multiple colors are used to create a pattern or picture. Each new color is added as indicated by the pattern, at which point the old color is dropped.

To work crochet intarsia, work the last loop of the last stitch (of the old color) using the new color (see Add a New Color on p. 110); bring both colors to the front to make sure they are in the correct position for the next row. Continue, using the new color only.

» Work over yarn tails (p. 111) whenever possible. This will save annoying hours of working them in at the end.

» Winding separate balls of each color will make working blocks easier. Make a sample block by working the number of stitches and rows required for your size, according to the first color block of the pattern (Row 3 below). Fasten off the sample, ravel it, and use it to measure lengths of each color for the remaining balls.

» Each color block is 10 (11, 12, 13) sts wide x 14 (15, 16, 17) rows long, however, during sleeve shaping the first and last color will not begin as a full color block.

coat

BACK

See Back construction diagram on p. 60 for assistance.

With H, ch 62 (68, 74, 80).

ROW 1 (RS): Hdc in 3rd ch from hook and in each ch across, change to I, turn—60 (66, 72, 78) hdc.

ROW 2: Ch 2, hdc across, turn. Fasten off I.

ROW 3 (SET UP FIRST ROW OF BLOCKS): With H, ch 2, hdc in first 10 (11, 12, 13) sts, join G, hdc in next 10 (11, 12, 13) sts, join C, hdc in next 10 (11, 12, 13) sts, join F, hdc in next 10 (11, 12, 13) sts, join E, hdc in next 10 (11, 12, 13) sts, join J, hdc in next 10 (11, 12, 13) sts, turn.

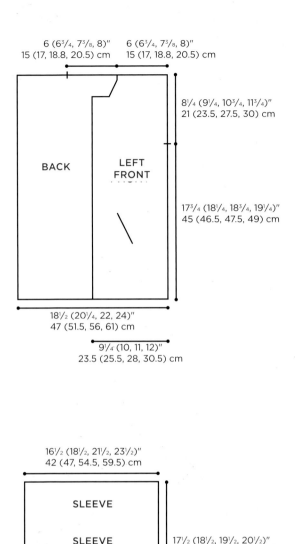

6 (6³/₄, 7³/₈, 8)"
15 (17, 18.8, 20.5) cm

6 (6³/₄, 7³/₈, 8)"
15 (17, 18.8, 20.5) cm

8¹/₄ (9¹/₄, 10³/₄, 11³/₄)"
21 (23.5, 27.5, 30) cm

BACK

LEFT FRONT

17³/₄ (18¹/₄, 18³/₄, 19¹/₄)"
45 (46.5, 47.5, 49) cm

18¹/₂ (20¹/₄, 22, 24)"
47 (51.5, 56, 61) cm

9¹/₄ (10, 11, 12)"
23.5 (25.5, 28, 30.5) cm

16¹/₂ (18¹/₂, 21¹/₂, 23¹/₂)"
42 (47, 54.5, 59.5) cm

SLEEVE

SLEEVE

17¹/₂ (18¹/₂, 19¹/₂, 20¹/₂)"
44.5 (47, 49.5, 52) cm

9¹/₄ (11, 13, 14³/₄)"
23.5 (28, 33, 37.5) cm

Work even in hdc, in intarsia, following colors as established in the prev row for 13 (14, 15, 16) more rows. Fasten off all colors.

Work 1 row in A. Work 1 row in F.

Work 2nd section of blocks as est in Row 3, using A, E, B, I, D, and C for 14 (15, 16, 17) rows.

Work 1 row in J. Work 1 row in B.

Work 3rd section of blocks, using D, I, F, H, J, and G for 14 (15, 16, 17) rows.

Work 1 row in E. Work 1 row in G.

Work 4th section of blocks, using J, C, E, B, A, and F for 14 (15, 16, 17) rows.

Work 1 row in H. Work 1 row in C.

Work 5th section of blocks, using G, A, H, D, I, and B for 13 (14, 15, 16) rows.

SHAPE SHOULDERS

Following color block patt on prev row, ch 2, hdc in first 20 (22, 24, 26) sts. Fasten off. Skip 20 (22, 24, 26) sts. Join yarn in next st, ch 2, hdc in same st, hdc across to end. Fasten off.

RIGHT FRONT

See Front construction diagram at right for assistance.

With H, ch 32 (35, 38, 41).

ROW 1 (RS): Hdc in 3rd ch from hook and in each ch across, change to I, turn—30 (33, 36, 39) hdc. Fasten off H.

ROW 2: Ch 2, hdc across, turn. Fasten off I.

ROW 3 (SET UP FIRST ROW OF BLOCKS): With F, ch 2, hdc in first 10 (11, 12, 13) sts, join E, hdc in next 10 (11, 12, 13) sts, join J, hdc in next 10 (11, 12, 13) sts, turn.

Work even in hdc, in intarsia, following colors as est in the prev row for 13 (14, 15, 16) more rows. Fasten off all colors.

Work 1 row in A. Work 1 row in F.

Work first 2 (3, 2, 3) rows of second section of blocks, using I, D, and C.

CONSTRUCTION DIAGRAMS

BACK

6 (6³/₄, 7³/₈, 8)"
15 (17, 18.8, 20.5) cm   6 (6³/₄, 7³/₈, 8)"
15 (17, 18.8, 20.5) cm

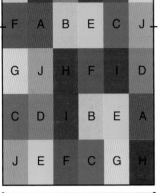

8¹/₄ (9¹/₄, 10³/₄, 11³/₄)"
21 (23.5, 27.5, 30) cm

18¹/₂ (19, 19¹/₄, 20)"
47 (48.5, 49, 51) cm

B	I	D	H	A	G
F	A	B	E	C	J
G	J	H	F	I	D
C	D	I	B	E	A
J	E	F	C	G	H

18¹/₂ (20¹/₄, 22, 24)"
47 (51.5, 56, 61) cm

9¹/₄ (10, 11, 12)"
23.5 (25.5, 28, 30.5) cm

SLEEVE

16¹/₂ (18¹/₂, 21¹/₂, 23¹/₂)"
42 (47, 54.5, 59.5) cm

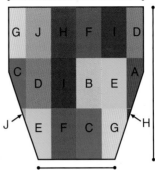

G	J	H	F	I	D
C	D	I	B	E	A
	E	F	C	G	

17¹/₂ (18¹/₂, 19¹/₂, 20¹/₂)"
44.5 (47, 49.5, 52) cm

J   H

9¹/₄ (11, 13, 14³/₄)"
23.5 (28, 33, 37.5) cm

FRONT

6 (6³/₄, 7³/₈, 8)"
15 (17, 18.8, 20.5) cm   6 (6³/₄, 7³/₈, 8)"
15 (17, 18.8, 20.5) cm

8¹/₄ (9¹/₄, 10³/₄, 11³/₄)"
21 (23.5, 27.5, 30) cm

18¹/₂ (19, 19¹/₄, 20)"
47 (48.5, 49, 51) cm

B	I	D	H	A	G
F	A	B	E	C	J
G	J	H	F	I	D
C	D	I	B	E	A
J	E	F	C	G	H

RIGHT FRONT 18¹/₂ (20¹/₄, 22, 24)" (47 [51.5, 56, 61] cm)

LEFT FRONT 9¹/₄ (10, 11, 12)" (23.5 [25.5, 28, 30.5] cm)

MAKE POCKET OUTSIDE

Ch 2, hdc across first block, hdc across 2nd block until only 3 sts remain, hdc2tog, hdc in last st of 2nd block, turn, leaving rem block un-worked—19 (21, 23, 25) hdc. Work 1 row even.

Work last 2 rows of pocket 5 (5, 6, 6) more times—14 (16, 17, 19) hdc.

MAKE POCKET LINING

With D, ch 22 (23, 24, 25). Work hdc into 3rd ch from hook, hdc into each ch across—20 (21, 22, 23) hdc.

Work even in hdc for 10 (10, 12, 12) more rows.

JOIN POCKET LINING TO BODY

With RS facing, join C with the last st, work across remaining block in C of Right Front, turn.

Work even in hdc for 11 (11, 13, 13) more rows using C and D as est.

Work 1 row in J, joining Pocket Lining to Pocket Outside by working through both layers at the same time. Work 1 row in B.

Work 3rd section of blocks, using H, J, and G for 14 (15, 16, 17) rows.

Work 1 row in E. Work 1 row in G.

Work 4th section of blocks, using B, A, and F for 14 (15, 16, 17) rows.

Work 1 row in H. Work 1 row in C.

Work 5th section of blocks, using D, I, and B for 4 (4, 6, 6) rows.

BEGIN NECK SHAPING

ROW 1 (RS): Sl st over first 5 (5, 6, 6) sts, hdc in next st, hdc2tog, hdc in each st across, turn—24 (27, 30, 33) hdc.

ROW 2: Work 1 row even.

ROW 3: Ch 2, hdc in same st, hdc2tog, hdc in each st across, turn—23 (26, 29, 32) hdc.

Rep last 2 rows 1 (1, 2, 2) more times—22 (25, 28, 31) hdc.

Work even until block section is complete. Fasten off.

LEFT FRONT

See Front construction diagram on p. 60 for assistance.

With H, ch 32, (35, 38, 41).

Work first 2 rows as for Right Front.

Work first section of blocks, using H, G, and C.

Work 1 row in A. Work 1 row in F.

Work first 2 (3, 2, 3) rows of 2nd section of blocks, using A, E, and B.

MAKE POCKET OUTSIDE

ROW 1 (RS): Drop A, skip all sts of first (A) block, pick up E, ch 2, hdc in first st, hdc2tog, hdc across E and B to end, turn—19 (21, 23, 25) hdc.

ROW 2: Work 1 row even.

Work last 2 rows of Pocket Outside 5 (5, 6, 6) more times—14 (16, 17, 19) hdc.

MAKE POCKET LINING

With E, ch 22 (23, 24, 25). Work hdc into 3rd ch from hook, hdc into each ch across—20 (21, 22, 23) hdc.

Work even in hdc for 10 (10, 12, 12) more rows.

JOIN POCKET LINING TO BODY

With RS facing, pick up A, work across color block A of Left Front, then continue across lining, turn.

Work even in hdc for 11 (11, 13, 13) more rows using A and E as est.

Work 1 row in J, joining Pocket Outside and Pocket Lining by working through both layers at the same time.

Work 1 row in B.

Work 3rd section of blocks, using D, I, and F for 14 (15, 16, 17) rows.

Work 1 row in E. Work 1 row in G.

Work 4th section of blocks, using J, C, and E for 14 (15, 16, 17) rows.

Work 1 row in H. Work 1 row in C.

Work 5th section of blocks, using G, A, and H for 4 (4, 6, 6) rows.

BEGIN NECK SHAPING

ROW 1 (RS): Ch 2, hdc across to last 8 (8, 9, 9) sts, hdc2tog, hdc, turn leaving rem sts unworked—24 (27, 30, 33) hdc.

ROW 2: Work 1 row even.

ROW 3: Ch 2, hdc across until 3 sts rem, hdc-2tog, hdc in last st—23 (26, 29, 32) hdc. Rep last 2 rows 1 (1, 2, 2) more time(s)—22 (25, 28, 31) hdc.

Work even until block section is complete. Fasten off.

SLEEVES (MAKE 2)

See Sleeve construction diagram on p. 60 for assistance.

With H, ch 32 (38, 44, 50).

ROW 1: Hdc into 3rd ch from hook and in each ch across, change to I, turn—30 (36, 42, 48) hdc.

ROWS 2-4: Work even in hdc, working 1 row each in I, D, and B.

BEGIN COLOR BLOCKS AND SLEEVE SHAPING

ROW 1: With G, ch 2, hdc in first st, 2 hdc in next st, hdc in next 3 (5, 7, 9) sts, switch to C, hdc in next 10 (11, 12, 13) sts, switch to F, hdc in next 10 (11, 12, 13) sts, switch to E, hdc in next 3 (5, 7, 9) sts, 2 hdc in next st, hdc in last st, turn—32 (38, 44, 50) hdc.

Cont to inc 1 st at beginning and end of every other row 8 (8, 9, 9) times; then every 4th row 3 (3, 4, 4) times, at the same time work color block patt as foll:

ROWS 2-10 (8, 6, 4): G, C, F, E.

ROWS 11 (9, 7, 5)-14 (15, 16, 17): H, G, C, F, E, J.

Work 1 row in A. Work 1 row in F.

Work second section of blocks, using A, E, B, I, D, and C for 14 (15, 16, 17) rows.

Work 1 row in K. Work 1 row in B.

Work 3rd section of blocks, using D, I, F, H, J, and G for 14 (15, 16, 17) rows—54 (60, 70, 76) hdc.

Work 1 row in E. Work 1 row in G. Fasten off.

FINISHING

Using mattress stitch (p. 117), sew shoulder seams together, sew Sleeves into armholes, sew sleeve seams, and side seams.

Sew lower edges of Pocket Linings to fronts on the wrong side, using whipstitch (p. 116).

COLLAR

With WS facing, join B to Left Front neck edge, where neck shaping begins, ch 2, hdc across neck to Right Front neck edge, working 1 hdc for each st and 1 st for each row, turn.

Work 1 row each in hdc in the foll color order: G, E, C, I, J, A, and H. Fasten off.

BUTTONBAND

With RS facing, join B to Left Front collar edge, ch 2, hdc down Left Front edge working 1 hdc for each row, ending at front bottom, turn. Work 1 row each in hdc in the foll color order: D, J, I, and H.

Fasten off.

BUTTONHOLE BAND

With RS facing, join B to bottom edge of Right Front, ch 2, hdc up Right Front edge working 1 hdc for each row, turn—88 (93, 98, 103) hdc. With D, hdc evenly across.

BEGIN BUTTONHOLE ROW

With K, hdc in first 6 (1, 7, 1) sts, *ch 1, skip 1 hdc, 9 hdc; rep from * 7 (8, 8, 9) more times, ending with hdc in last 2 sts.

Work 1 row in I, working hdc in each ch-sp of buttonhole row. Work 1 row in H. Fasten off.

Using buttonholes as a guide, sew buttons onto Buttonband with needle and thread. Weave in loose ends, then gently steam block (p. 118) to final measurements.

AUTUMN SUN *wrap/scarf*

finished size

18" (45.5 cm) wide x 72" (183 cm) long, after blocking.

yarn

Fingering weight (#1 Super Fine) in red, burgundy, and orange.

SHOWN: Zitron Trekking XXL (75% superwash wool, 25% nylon; 459 yd [420 m]/3.75 oz [100 g]): #146 red twist (A); #147 wine twist (B), 2 skeins each; #145 orange twist (C), 1 skein.

hook

G/6 (4 mm) or size needed to obtain gauge.

notions

Tapestry needle.

gauge

Larger motif measures 6" (15 cm) across, smaller motif measures 2" (5 cm) across.

I don't make socks. Ever. I rely on friends who like knitting socks to give them to me as gifts. But sock yarn is such a wonderful choice for crochet. It's the perfect weight, and there are so many choices of yarn in so many gorgeous colors. This wrap/scarf was inspired by these fairly muted autumnal colors of sock yarn. They seemed a gifted match for the sunlike motif in the wrap/scarf.

notes

» This wrap/scarf is made up of the same large motif, worked alternately in two colors to create a checkerboard. The motifs are attached as the wrap is worked.

» Make one full motif, then join remaining motifs on last round as you go. Each motif is joined by three points to the next motif.

» Make and join one small motif in between two large motifs, attaching to one point before a join, one joined point of one motif, one joined point of next motif, and one point after the second join.

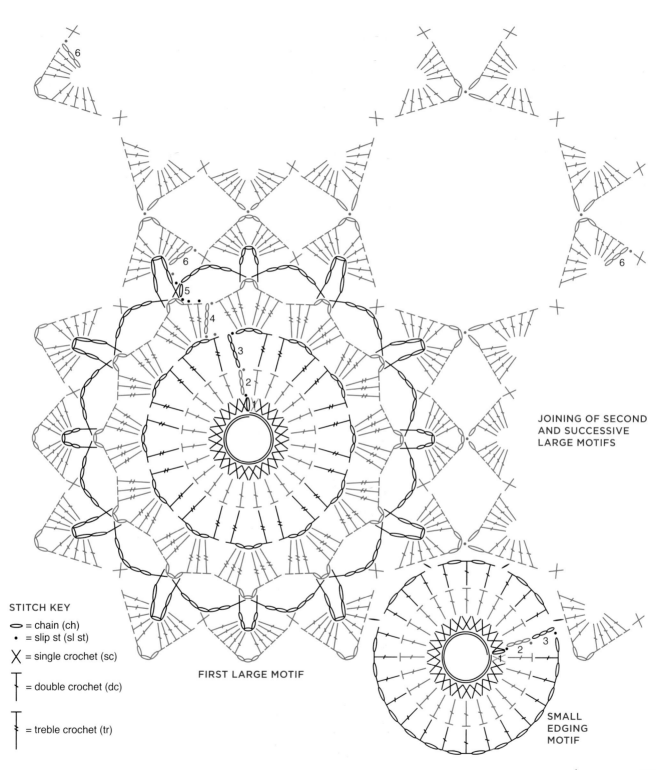

6

6

6

5

4

3

2

1

JOINING OF SECOND
AND SUCCESSIVE
LARGE MOTIFS

STITCH KEY

◯ = chain (ch)

• = slip st (sl st)

✕ = single crochet (sc)

┃ = double crochet (dc)

╪ = treble crochet (tr)

FIRST LARGE MOTIF

3

2

1

**SMALL
EDGING
MOTIF**

wrap/scarf

See stitch diagram on p. 67 for assistance.

FIRST LARGE MOTIF

With A, make adjustable ring (p. 122).

RND 1: Work 24 sc into loop; sl st in first sc to join—24 sc.

RND 2: Ch 3 (counts as first dc), dc in each sc around, sl st in top of beg ch-3 to join.

RND 3: Ch 4 (counts as first tr), tr in next dc, *ch 3, tr in next 2 dc; rep from * around, ending with ch-3, sl st in top of beg ch-4 to join—12 ch-sps.

RND 4: Sl st in next tr of prev rnd, sl st into first ch-3 sp, ch 4 (counts as first tr), (2 tr, ch 3, 3 tr) into same ch-3 sp, (3 tr, ch 3, 3 tr) into each ch-3 sp around, sl st in 4th ch of beg ch-4 to join.

RND 5: Sl st in next 2 tr, sl st into first ch-3 sp, ch 1, (sc, ch 5, sc) in same ch-sp, ch 5, *(sc, ch 5, sc) into next ch-3 sp, ch 5; rep from * around, sl st in first sc of rnd.

RND 6: Sl st into first ch-5 sp, ch 3 (counts as first dc), work (4 dc, ch 3, 5 dc) into same sp, sc into next ch-5 sp, *(5 dc, ch 3, 5 dc) into next ch-5 sp, sc into next ch-5 sp; rep from * around, sl st in top of beg ch-3 to join. Fasten off.

SECOND LARGE MOTIF

With B, work as for First Large Motif through Rnd 5.

JOINING RND 6: Sl st into first ch-5 sp, ch 3 (counts as first dc), (4 dc, ch 3, 5 dc) into same sp, sc into next ch-5 sp, *[(5 dc, ch 1, sl st into corresponding ch-3 sp of prev motif, ch 1, 5 dc) into next ch-5 sp, sc into next ch-5 sp] 3 times, cont around as for Rnd 6 of First Large Motif, joining 3 points for each motif as necessary.

Following construction diagram at right, make and join motifs, alternating A and B, in rows of 3 motifs wide x 12 motifs long.

SMALL EDGING MOTIFS

With C, make adjustable ring.

RND 1: Work 24 sc into loop, sl st in first sc to join—24 sc.

RND 2: Ch 3 (counts as first dc), dc in each sc, sl st to top of beg ch-3 to join.

RND 3: Ch 3, sl st to center dc of large motif point before a joining point, *[dc in next dc, ch 1] twice, dc in next dc*, sl st in center dc on side edge of a joined point on same large motif, rep from * to * once, sl st in center dc on side edge of a joined point on next large motif, [dc in next dc, ch 1] twice, dc in next dc, sl st in center dc of next point after a joining point, (dc in next dc, ch 1) around small motif, sl st in top of beg ch-3 to join. Fasten off.

Make and join a total of 26 small motifs, attaching one in between two joined large motifs along edge of wrap (see construction diagram at right for assistance).

FINISHING

Weave in loose ends. Block wrap by machine washing in cold water on gentle cycle and then dry on low until almost dry.

CONSTRUCTION DIAGRAM

DIAGRAM KEY
A = LARGE MOTIF IN A
B = LARGE MOTIF IN B
C = SMALL MOTIF IN C

URCHINS and LIMPETS *blanket*

finished size

48" (122 cm) long x 36" (91.5 cm) wide, including border.

yarn

Worsted weight (#4 Medium) in light gray, medium green, orange, muted yellow, muted violet, dark green, dark gray-brown, muted blue, and rust-brown.

SHOWN: Mission Falls 1824 Wool (100% superwash merino wool; 85 yd [78 m]/1.75 oz [50 g]): #006 oatmeal (MC), 12 balls; #028 pistachio (C), 2 balls; #026 zinnia (A); # 014 dijon (B); #025 mallow (D); #018 spruce (E); #008 earth (F); #020 cornflower (G); #012 raisin (H), 1 ball each.

hook

J/10 (6 mm) or size needed to obtain gauge.

notions

Tapestry needle.

gauge

Each background motif measures 7³/₄" (19.5 cm) square.

Each center motif measures 3¹/₂" (9 cm) square.

The background motifs of this blanket remind me of sea urchins, and the cheery centers remind me of limpet shells. In the background motif, the single crochet sections increase every round, and the chain spaces remain the same. In the small circles, the chain spaces increase with each round, and the single crochets stay the same. It's a simple concept that, nonetheless, creates a lovely, cozy blanket. Any other combination of neutral background and pops of color would work well. Or change the feeling altogether and use a deep burnt orange as the background and stone gray, charcoal, bottle green, and navy for contrast.

» Motifs are worked with the right side always facing. Do not turn at the end of each round.

» After first motif is completed, all subsequent motifs are worked through Rnd 7 as for First Background Motif, then joined to each other during Rnd 8, connecting two chain spaces for each side.

urchins and limpets blanket

Refer to the construction diagram on p. 74 for assistance.

FIRST BACKGROUND MOTIF

With MC, make an adjustable ring (p. 122).

RND 1: Ch 1, 16 sc into loop, sl st in first sc of rnd—16 sc.

RND 2: Ch 1, *sc, ch 5, skip 1 sc; rep from * around, ending with sl st in first sc of rnd—8 ch-sps.

RND 3: Sl st twice into first ch-sp, sc in same ch-sp, ch 4, *sc into next ch-sp, ch 4; rep from * around, ending with sc in first sc of rnd.

RND 4: Ch 1, sc into side of last sc of prev rnd, sc in next sc, *(sc, ch 4, sc) into next ch-sp, sc in next sc; rep from * around ending with sc in last ch-sp, ch 3, sc into side of first sc—3 sc in each section.

RND 5: Ch 1, sc into side of last sc of prev rnd, sc in each sc to ch-sp, *(sc, ch 4, sc) into next ch-sp, sc in each sc to ch-sp; rep from * around ending with sc in last ch-sp, ch 3, sc into side of first sc—5 sc in each section.

RNDS 6–8: Work as for Rnd 5, inc 2 sc in each section, until there are 11 sc in each section. Fasten off.

MOTIFS 2–30

Following the stitch diagram at right, make and join each motif across a row in turn, following First Background Motif through Rnd 7, then joining one or two sides as follows:

JOINING ONE SIDE:

RND 8: Ch 1, sc into side of last sc of prev rnd, sc in each sc to ch-sp, *(sc, ch 2, sl st in ch-sp of prev motif, ch 2, sc) into next ch-sp, sc in each sc to ch-sp; rep from * once, cont rnd as for First Background Motif—11 sc in each section.

JOINING TWO SIDES:

RND 8: Ch 1, sc into side of last sc of prev rnd, sc in each sc to ch-sp, *(sc, ch 2, sl st in ch-sp of prev motif, ch 2, sc) into next ch-sp, sc in each sc to ch-sp; rep from * once, rep from * for second adjoining motif twice, cont rnd as for First Background Motif—11 sc in each section.

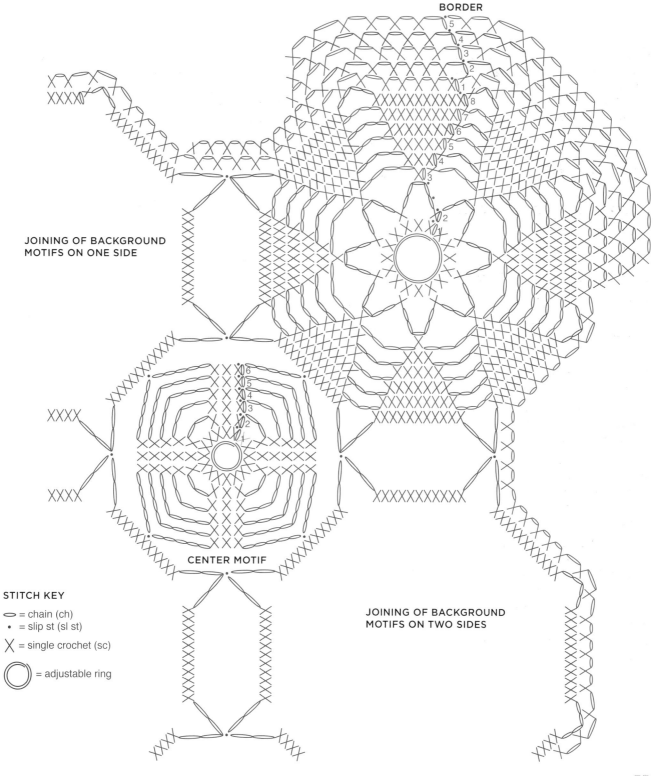

BORDER

5
4
3
2
1
8
7
6
5
4
3
2
1

JOINING OF BACKGROUND
MOTIFS ON ONE SIDE

6
5
4
3
2
1

CENTER MOTIF

JOINING OF BACKGROUND
MOTIFS ON TWO SIDES

STITCH KEY

⬭ = chain (ch)

• = slip st (sl st)

✕ = single crochet (sc)

◯ = adjustable ring

FIRST CENTER MOTIF

With E, make an adjustable ring.

RND 1: Ch 1, 16 sc into loop, sl st in first sc to join—16 sc.

RND 2: Ch 1, sc in first 3 sc, ch 2, skip next sc, *sc in next 3 sc, ch 2, skip next sc; rep from * around, sl st in first sc to join—4 ch-2 sps.

RND 3: Ch 1, *sc in each sc to next ch-sp, ch 4; rep from * around, sl st in first sc to join—4 ch-4 sps.

RNDS 4–5: Work as for Rnd 3, inc 2 ch in each corner on every rnd ending with 4 ch-8 sps.

RND 6 (JOINING RND): Ch 1, *sc in each sc to next ch-sp, ch 5, sl st in 6th sc of one side of a background motif, ch 5; rep from * around, attaching each side of First Center Motif to one side of surrounding background motifs.

Following Color Guide at top right, cont making Center Motifs, working in rows, beginning at top right corner of blanket.

BORDER

Join H in ch-sp of upper right background motif, ch 1, for each sc section work as follows: [sc in next sc, ch 1, skip next sc] 5 times, sc in last sc, ch 1, for each ch-sp work as follows: [sc, ch 1] twice, work in patt around blanket, sc in first sc to join.

RND 2: With B, ch 2, work (sc into next ch-sp, ch 1) around blanket, sl st in beg ch-2 sp to join.

RNDS 3–5: Rep Rnd 2 using G, D, and then C. Fasten off.

FINISHING

Weave in ends. Gently handwash blanket in cool water and wet block (p. 118) to final measurements.

color guide:

TOP ROW: E, H, B, A.

SECOND ROW: A, D, E, F.

THIRD ROW: F, H, C, D.

FOURTH ROW: G, B, A, E.

FIFTH ROW: C, F, H, G.

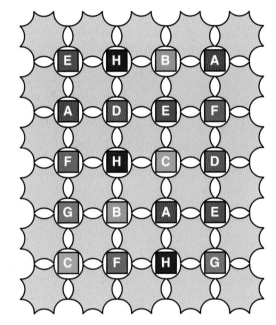

CONSTRUCTION DIAGRAM

COLOR *adventures*

The previous chapters introduced you to several different ways of working with color. This chapter contains projects that will help you take what you've learned and use it to create slightly more advanced projects. The Triangles Tuffet on p. 87 will challenge you to work with a large number of colors in one piece. Mastering an extensive color scheme may take a little practice, but it opens up a world of possibilities. In contrast to the careful planning of the Triangles Tuffet color scheme, the Circles Table Topper on p. 99 is a study in making random colors work together. Once you have mastered the concept, try picking just a handful of colors at random, even throwing in a few you don't love—embrace the challenge and satisfaction of creating something organized and beautiful out of a random smattering of colors.

I hope the projects in the following pages will encourage you to be even more adventurous with color and inspire you to explore your crochet skills further. Have fun, delve into color and, of course, play with yarn. Doing so has kept me busy and happy for many years.

CLOVER *hat*

finished size

20" (51 cm) circumference x 9" (23 cm) long.

yarn

Worsted weight (#4 Medium) in light green/yellow and fuchsia.

SHOWN: Malabrigo Merino Worsted (100% merino wool; 216 yd [198 m]/3.5 oz [100 g]): #126 brillante (A); #125 mariposa (B), 1 skein each.

hook

J/10 (6 mm) or size needed to obtain gauge.

notions

Tapestry needle.

gauge

14 sts x 14 rows = 4" (10 cm) in sc blo in the round.

Malabrigo worsted yarn is amazingly soft and is dyed in rich colors that make me swoon. The pretty clover design on this cozy hat would work with solid colors, but if you cheat a bit and use two slightly variegated colors, you can enjoy the crocheting and watch as the pattern emerges. For this to be effective, you need to choose two colors that are fairly contrasting and don't share the same hues.

notes

» Hat is worked in joined rounds with the right side always facing you. Begin each round with one chain to count as the first stitch. Continue to follow the pattern chart (below) working in single crochet through the back loops only and end each round with a slip stitch in the first chain to join.

» This color pattern is achieved with the color not in use stranded (p. 113) across the back. When working a round that does not have color changes, simply drop the color not in use at the beginning of the round and pick it up again on the next round.

hat

BODY

With A, ch 70, sl st in first ch to form circle, being careful not to twist. Follow the pattern chart below for 28 rnds.

SHAPE CROWN

RND 1: With B, ch 1, skip first 2 sts, sc2tog around, sl st in beg ch-1 to join—35 sts.

RND 2: With A, ch 1, skip first st, sc2tog around, sl st in beg ch-1 to join—18 sts.

RND 3: With B, ch 1, skip first 2 sts, sc2tog around—9 sts. Fasten off, leaving a tail for sewing. With tapestry needle, use tail to gather remaining sts and pull to close hole. Fasten off. Weave in ends.

BOTTOM EDGE

With WS facing, join A and B to first ch loop of Rnd 1. With A, ch 1, *change to B, sc in next st, change to A, sc in next st; rep from * around, ending with B, sl st in beg ch-1 to join. Fasten off. Weave in ends.

PATTERN CHART

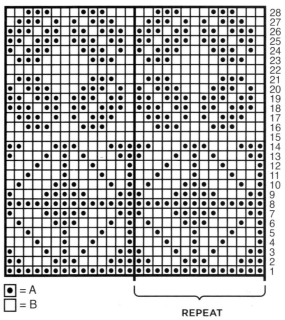

● = A
□ = B

REPEAT

SWIRLS *pillow*

finished size

13" x 10" (33 x 25.5 cm).

yarn

Worsted weight (#4 Medium) in dark blue, mint green, tan, and red.

SHOWN: Fibre Company Terra (60% merino, 20% baby alpaca, 20% silk; 100 yd [90 m]/1.75 oz [50 g]): medium indigo (MC), 2 skeins; mint (A); iron (B); madder (C); 1 skein each.

hook

J/10 (6 mm) or size needed to obtain gauge.

notions

Tapestry needle; about 12 oz (350 g) fiberfill for stuffing.

gauge

17 sts x 12 rows = 4" (10 cm).

The colorwork pattern on this bold pillow reminds me of carvings in old French churches and heraldic emblems. Although brighter colors are featured here, using a muted palette of black and ecru or going with tweedy cement shades would be even more reminiscent of a carving in an ancient building. The back of the pillow is worked in simple rectangles of color, giving you a chance to rest from reading the chart.

notes

» This color pattern is achieved with the color not in use stranded (p. 113) across the back. Catch strands every four stitches to prevent pulling. Carry the strands loosely to keep fabric from puckering.

» The pillow is made in joined rounds working through the back loops only. The first chain at the beginning of the round does not count as a stitch.

swirls pillow

With A, ch 43.

RND 1: Beg in 2nd ch from hook, follow swirl chart for front across, working across the opposite side of foundation ch, follow color block chart for back, sl st in first sc to join—84 sc.

RNDS 2–47: Ch 1, foll Front color chart and Back color chart at right, working in sc blo, sl st in first sc to join.

RND 48: Ch 1, foll Front color chart across, join front and back tog as foll: [with C, sc blo in next st, sl st in corresponding st of front] 7 times, cont with Back color chart until 7 sts from end, [with MC, sc blo in next st, sl st in corresponding st of front] 7 times, sl st in first sc to join. Fasten off. Leave a long tail of MC for sewing up.

FINISHING

Weave in loose ends. Gently steam block (p. 118) pillow to finished measurements.

Use fiberfill to stuff pillow firmly. With tapestry needle and MC, sew opening shut stitch by stitch using herringbone stitch (p. 116). Tuck in small amounts of fiberfill as you sew to make sure the stuffing fills the upper edge of the pillow.

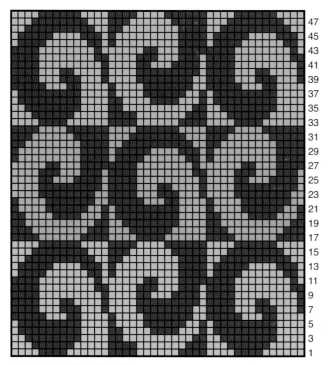

FRONT COLOR CHART
Every other row labeled.

47
45
43
41
39
37
35
33
31
29
27
25
23
21
19
17
15
13
11
9
7
5
3
1

BACK COLOR CHART
Every other row labeled.

47
45
43
41
39
37
35
33
31
29
27
25
23
21
19
17
15
13
11
9
7
5
3
1

TRIANGLES *tuffet*

finished size

21″ (48.5 cm) diameter x 10″ (25.5 cm) high.

yarn

Chunky weight (# 6 Bulky) in dark blue, lavender, orange, dark green, persimmon, brown, chartreuse, magenta, forest green, and yellow.

SHOWN*: Crystal Palace Deco Ribbon (70% acrylic, 30% nylon; 80 yd [70 m]/1.8 oz [50 g]): #116 magenta/blue (A); #103 black/cobalt (B); #115 periwinkle/magenta (C); #122 jade/lime (D); #211 berry lemon (E), #124 red/cobalt (F); #204 flaming poppy (G); #118 kiwi/orange (H); #108 dark green/kiwi stripe (I); #126 lemon/kiwi (J), 2 balls each.

* Unfortunately a few of the colors listed above are no longer produced. These are the recommended substitutions: for #115 periwinkle/magenta, substitute #123 purple/magenta; for #122 jade/lime, substitute #9541 scuba dive; for # 118 kiwi/orange, substitute #434 kiwi/mango; for #108 dark green/kiwi stripe, substitute #319 lettuce.

hook

J/10 (6 mm) or size needed to obtain gauge.

notions

About 48 oz (1,361 g) fiberfill; long straight pins; tapestry needle.

gauge

Each triangle of Big Circles measures 1″ (2.5 cm) at the narrowest point, 6″ (15 cm) at the outer edge, and 9″ (23 cm) at each long side.

Pouf? Ottoman? Footstool? Any of these terms can be used to describe this round stuffed cylinder for resting your feet while you crochet. It's loud and colorful but could easily be made in quiet tasteful shades to match your décor. My inspiration was the classic idea of a Victorian study inhabited by fez-sporting gents in smoking jackets, who of course need somewhere to rest their tired feet.

notes

» Turning chain does not count as a stitch.

» The Side Piece is constructed of triangles that reverse direction at every color change to make a rectangular shape.

tuffet

BIG CIRCLE (MAKE 2)

See stitch diagram A below for assistance.

FIRST CIRCLE:
Work in the foll color order: I, G, E, D, H, B, F, C, J, A.

SECOND CIRCLE:
Work in the foll color order: J, I, A, H, E, F, D, G, B, C.

With first color, ch 29.

ROW 1: Sl st in 2nd ch from hook and next 6 ch, sc in next 7 ch, hdc in next 7 ch, dc in last 7 ch, turn—28 sts.

ROW 2: Ch 3, dc in first 7 dc, hdc in next 7 hdc, sc in next 7 sc, sl st in last 7 sl st, turn.

ROW 3: Ch 1, sl st in first 7 sl st, sc in next 7 sc, hdc in next hdc, dc in last 7 dc, turn.

ROWS 4–11: Rep Rows 2 and 3 four times.

DIAGRAM A

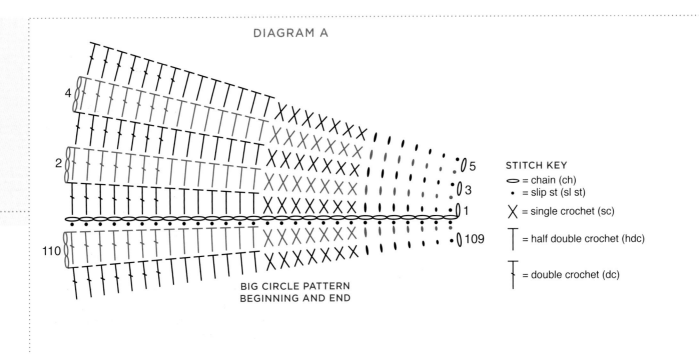

BIG CIRCLE PATTERN
BEGINNING AND END

STITCH KEY

⬯ = chain (ch)

• = slip st (sl st)

✕ = single crochet (sc)

┬ = half double crochet (hdc)

╤ = double crochet (dc)

DIAGRAM B

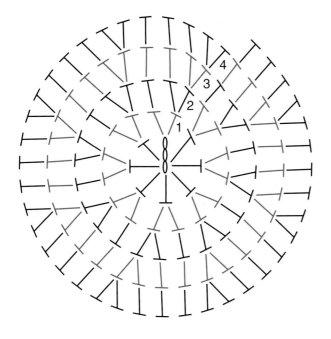

Change color and work Rows 2 and 3 five times, then Row 2 once again.

Continue in patt as est, changing color every 11 rows, until you have 10 triangular sections. To close circle, hold first and last section together. Working through both layers, sl st in each st across. Fasten off. Weave in ends.

CENTER CIRCLES
(MAKE 1 WITH B, 1 WITH F)

See stitch diagram B at left for assistance.

Ch 3, 8 hdc in 3rd ch from hook, do not join to beg of rnd, cont around in a spiral fashion.

RND 1: [2 hdc in next hdc] 8 times—16 hdc.

RND 2: [2 hdc in next hdc, hdc in next hdc] 8 times—24 hdc.

RND 3: [2 hdc in next hdc, hdc in next 2 hdc] 8 times—32 hdc.

RND 4: [2 hdc in next hdc, hdc in next 3 hdc] 8 times—40 hdc. Fasten off, leaving a long tail for sewing up.

SIDE PIECE

Begin with B, then change colors in the foll order as directed below: F, G, I, E, H, F, D, B, H, A, D, I, J, G, E, A, B, C, H, D, F, D, I, A, J.

FIRST TRIANGLE

ROW 1: With B, ch 33, sl st in 2nd ch from hook and next 7 ch, sc in next 8 ch, hdc in next 8 ch, dc in last 8 ch, turn—32 sts.

ROW 2: Ch 3, dc in each dc, hdc in each hdc, sc in each sc, sl st in each sl st, turn.

ROW 3: Ch 1, sl st in each sl st, sc in each sc, hdc in each hdc, dc in each dc across, turn.

ROWS 4-7: Rep Rows 2 and 3 twice, turn.

Change color and work Rows 3 and 2 three times, then Row 3 once more.

Continue in est patt, changing color as directed above until there are 26 triangles. Fasten off. Weave in ends. Do not sew ends together to allow for stuffing.

FINISHING

Pin 1 Center Circle to fill opening at center of 1 Big Circle. With tapestry needle, use long tail to sew circle in place on WS with mattress stitch (p. 117). Repeat for second circles. With RS together, pin outer edge of Big Circle to one edge of Side Piece, gently stretching if necessary. With tapestry needle and B, sew top and side together with mattress stitch. Stuff Tuffet with fiberfill, using enough to make a firm cushion. Pin and sew remaining Big Circle to Side Piece as before.

Once top and bottom have been attached, add more stuffing until Tuffet is completely filled and has no obvious empty spots.

Sew up side opening with mattress stitch.

SPLASHY *flowers scarf*

finished size

72" (183 cm) long x 13½" (34.5 cm) wide.

yarn

Worsted weight (#4 Medium) in lime/yellow/olive/orange/magenta and lime/pink/red/purple/orange/rust.

SHOWN: Noro Silk Garden (45% silk, 45% kid mohair, 10% lambswool; 108 yd [98 m]/1.75 oz [50 g]): #255 lime/yellow/olive/orange/magenta (A) 3 skeins, #258 lime/pink/red/purple/orange/rust (B), 2 skeins.

hook

H/8 (5 mm) or size needed to obtain gauge.

gauge

Each Large Flower measures 4½" (11.5 cm) square after washing.

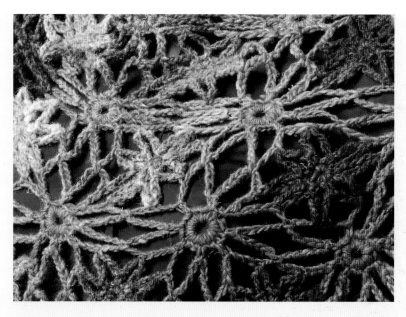

The long color repeats of these Noro fiber-dyed yarns make this scarf gloriously colorful and also make it look more complicated than it really is. There are only two different colorways used, one for the large flowers and one for the small flowers. Both of the flower motifs are quite simple to make, yet the colors of the yarn change from pale gold to pink, purple, and green, and end with brown, giving the motifs more depth. You'd be just as successful choosing two colorways of blue and yellow or red, orange, and brown.

notes

» The scarf is made up of Large and Small Flower motifs with petals made of chain spaces.

» Begin by making and joining the Large Corner, Large Side, and Large Flower motifs according to the construction diagram on p.96 (see also Assemble Scarf on p. 96), working across in rows.

» After all of the Main Motifs are joined, fill in the spaces between motifs with Small Flowers by joining each petal to the side of a Large Flower petal.

LARGE SIDE FLOWER

LARGE FLOWER

SMALL FLOWER

LARGE CORNER FLOWER

LARGE SIDE FLOWER

STITCH KEY

⬯ = chain (ch)
• = slip st (sl st)
X = single crochet (sc)
T = half double crochet (hdc)

scarf

Refer to the stitch diagram at left for assistance.

MAIN MOTIFS

LARGE FLOWER (MAKE 30):

RND 1: With A (or B), ch 3 (counts as first hdc), 15 hdc into 3rd ch from hook, sl st in first hdc to join—16 hdc.

RND 2: Ch 15 (counts as first sc, ch 14), *skip next hdc, sc in next hdc, ch 14; rep from * around, ending with sl st in first sc at beg of rnd—8 petals. Fasten off.

LARGE CORNER FLOWER (MAKE 4):

RND 1: With A (or B), ch 3 (counts as first hdc), 15 hdc into 3rd ch from hook, sl st in first hdc to join—16 hdc.

RND 2: Ch 15 (counts as first sc, ch 14), *skip next hdc, sc in next hdc, ch 14; rep from * 2 times, skip next hdc, sc in next hdc—4 petals. Fasten off.

LARGE SIDE FLOWER (MAKE 34):

RND 1: With A (or B), ch 3 (counts as first hdc), 15 hdc into 3rd ch from hook, sl st in first hdc to join—16 hdc.

RND 2: Ch 15 (counts as first sc, ch 14), *skip next hdc, sc in next hdc, ch 14; rep from * 4 times, skip next hdc, sc in next hdc—6 petals. Fasten off.

SMALL FLOWER (MAKE 48):

RND 1: With A (or B), ch 3 (counts as first hdc), 7 hdc in 3rd ch from hook, sl st in first hdc to join—8 hdc.

RND 2: Ch 5 (counts as first sc, ch 4), sl st to side of one Large Flower petal bordering space, ch 4, *sc in next hdc, (ch 4, sl st to side of next Large Flower petal bordering space, ch 4); rep from * around, ending with sl st in first sc at beg of rnd—8 petals. Fasten off.

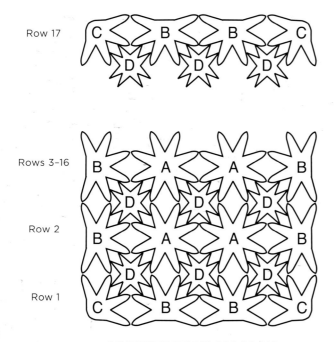

Row 17

Rows 3–16

Row 2

Row 1

CONSTRUCTION DIAGRAM

JOINING

JOINING ONE SIDE:

Work as for specified flower through Rnd 1.

RND 2: Ch 15 (counts as first sc, ch 14), skip next hdc, sc in next hdc, [ch 7, sl st to corresponding ch-14 sp of prev flower, ch 7, skip next hdc, sc in next hdc] twice, finish flower as for Rnd 2 of motif.

JOINING TWO SIDES:

Work as for specified flower through Rnd 1.

RND 2: Ch 15 (counts as first sc, ch 14), skip next hdc, sc in next hdc, [ch 7, sl st to corresponding ch-14 sp of first adjoining flower, ch 7, skip next hdc, sc in next hdc] twice, [ch 7, sl st to corresponding ch-14 sp of next adjoining flower, ch 7, skip next hdc, sc in next hdc] twice, finish flower as for Rnd 2 of motif.

ASSEMBLE SCARF

Begin with 1 complete Large Corner Flower. Following the layout in the construction diagram above, and working across in rows, make and join each flower motif using instructions to Join One or Two Sides as needed.

FINISHING

Weave in loose ends. Machine wash in cold water with soap for delicates on handwash cycle (if your machine has one) or on gentle cycle. This will remove excess vegetable matter and make the scarf soft. If you don't trust your machine, handwash instead.

Lay flat to dry, gently pulling to finished measurements.

CIRCLES *table topper*

finished size

29" (73.5cm) in diameter.

yarn

Laceweight (#0 Lace) in light yellow-green, dark blue-green, medium gray, green, medium blue, aqua, dark baby blue, light green, blue-green, chartreuse, light tan, navy blue, very dark green, dark green, tan, light gold, medium blue, medium muted blue, orange, forest green, and light blue.

SHOWN: DMC #5 Perle Cotton Thread (100% mercerized cotton; 27 yd [2 5 m]/.2 oz [5 g]): #3348 lt. yellow green (A), 5 skeins; #0500 very dk. blue green (B); #0642 dk. beige gray (C); #0699 green (D); #0798 dk. delft blue (E); #0807 peacock blue (F), 4 skeins each; #0312 very dk. baby blue (G); #0368 lt. pistachio green (H); #0502 blue green (I); #0703 chartreuse (J); #0739 ultra very lt. tan (K); #0823 dk. navy blue (L); #0890 ultra dk. pistachio green (M), 3 skeins each; #0319 very dk pistachio green (N); #0367 dk. pistachio green (O); #0437 lt. tan (P); #0676 lt. old gold (Q); #0799 med. delft blue (R); #0931 med. antique blue (S); #0976 med. golden brown (T); #0988 med. forest green (U); #3325 lt. baby blue (V), 2 skeins each.

hook

D/3 (3.25 mm) or size needed to obtain gauge.

notions

Tapestry needle.

gauge

Each circle motif measures 3 1/4" (8.5 cm) diameter.

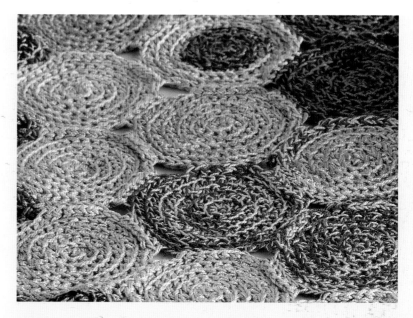

"Blue and green should never be seen" is an old-fashioned caution that doesn't really make much sense. Many color combinations work beautifully when they are balanced by using several shades of each color, along with just a bit of neutral to tie everything together. The inspiration for this piece came from a flat slate patio composed of small regular shapes. When I saw all of these exciting shades of blue and green yarn, I knew I had found my color palette in spite of that silly old adage about blue and green.

notes

» Table topper is made with two strands of yarn held together.

» Two strands held together may get out of synch. Extra skeins may be needed, or you may have some extra yarn left over. If you are concerned about running out of yarn, you may want to purchase an extra skein just to be safe.

» All stitches are worked through back loops only.

» Motifs are worked in spiral fashion, without joining rounds.

» Each motif is joined to the previous one on Rnd 6. Join first six stitches to the previous motif, work two stitches on the working motif without joining, and then join the next six stitches to corresponding stitches on the next motif as necessary. Some motifs will only be joined to one motif, while others may be joined to two or three motifs.

» Each joined section will have two unjoined stitches between them.

circles table topper

Make 2 balls of yarn—1 in each of the Color Orders listed below. Begin with first color, roll into a ball, add next color by knotting the ends of each color together with a square knot (p. 121), and continue rolling the ball. Continue to join and roll each color in the Color Order. Use 1 strand of each ball held together to make motifs.

COLOR ORDER 1: 0798 (E), 0739 (K), 0699 (D), 0807 (F), 0703 (J), 0500 (B), 0798 (E), 0368 (H), 0642 (C), 0799 (R), 0703 (J), 0739 (K), 0336, 0890 (M), 3325 (V), 0699 (D), 0807 (F), 0368 (H), 0319 (N), 0437 (P), 0312 (G), 0988 (U), 0642 (C), 3348 (A), 0976 (T), 0500 (B), 0931 (S), 0502 (I), 0676 (Q), 03348 (A), 0823 (L), 0798 (E), 0367 (O).

COLOR ORDER 2: 0890 (M), 0502 (I), 0312 (G), 0823 (L), 0699 (D), 0807 (F), 03348 (A), 0500 (B), 3348 (A), 0890 (M), 0642 (C), 0312 (G), 0988 (U), 0931 (S), 0807 (F), 0676 (Q), 3348 (A), 0500 (B), 0799 (R), 0739 (K), 0367 (O), 0823 (L), 0502 (I), 0798 (E), 0336, 0699 (D), 0437 (P), 0642 (C), 0703 (J), 3325 (V), 0319 (N), 0368 (H), 0976 (T).

See stitch diagram on p. 101 for assistance with First Motif and Remaining Motifs.

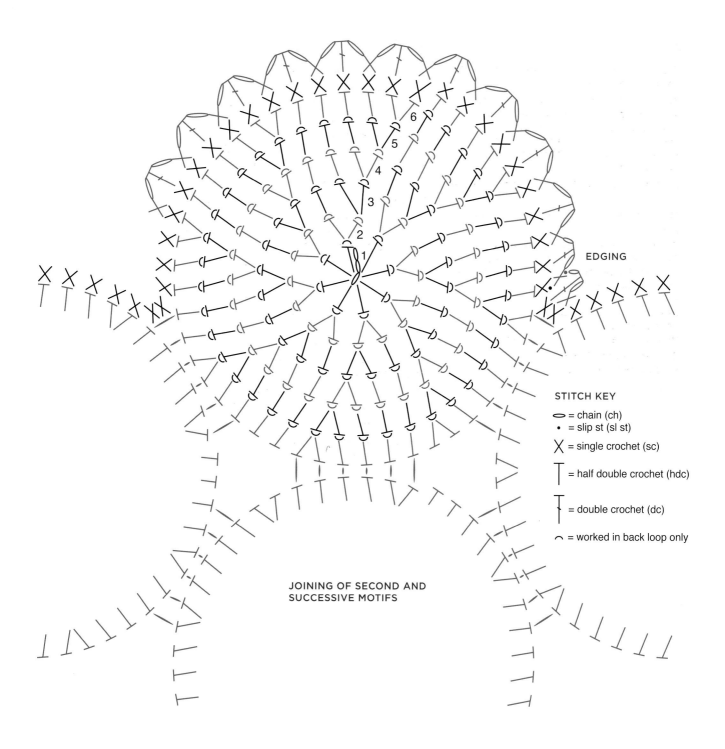

EDGING

STITCH KEY

⬭ = chain (ch)

• = slip st (sl st)

X = single crochet (sc)

T = half double crochet (hdc)

T = double crochet (dc)

⌒ = worked in back loop only

JOINING OF SECOND AND
SUCCESSIVE MOTIFS

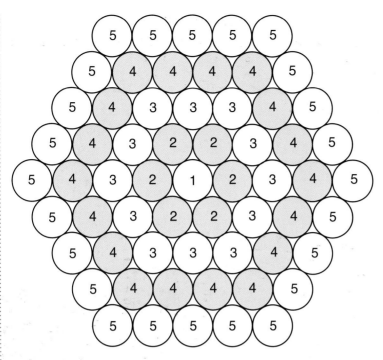

CONSTRUCTION DIAGRAM

FIRST MOTIF

With 1 strand of each ball held together, ch 3.

RND 1: 8 hdc blo in 3rd ch from hook.

RND 2: 2 hdc blo in each hdc around—16 hdc.

RND 3: [2 hdc blo in next hdc, hdc blo in next hdc] 8 times—24 hdc.

RND 4: [2 hdc blo in next hdc, hdc blo in each of next 2 hdc] 8 times—32 hdc.

RND 5: [2 hdc blo in next hdc, hdc blo in each of next 3 hdc] 8 times—40 hdc.

RND 6: [2 hdc blo in next hdc, hdc blo in each of next 4 hdc] 8 times—48 hdc. Fasten off.

REMAINING MOTIFS

JOINING RND 6: [hdc blo, sl st in next st on previous motif] twice in next st on working motif, [hdc blo in next st, sl st in next st on previous motif] 4 times, hdc blo in next 2 sts without joining, continue as for Rnd 6 of First Motif joining additional motifs in the same manner as necessary (see Notes on p. 100). Fasten off.

Following the construction diagram above, begin with First Motif as the center, make and join 6 motifs surrounding first motif for Round 2, 12 motifs for Round 3, 18 motifs for Round 4, and then 24 motifs for Round 5.

EDGING

With 1 strand of each ball held together, join yarn between 2 motifs on outer edge. Sc evenly around, working sc in each st and 2 sc in each join.

NEXT RND: *(Sc, ch 1) in next sc, (dc, ch 1) in next sc; rep from * around, sl st in first sc to join.

Fasten off. Weave in ends.

FINISHING

Steam block (p. 118) the finished piece gently to smooth and shape.

TINY MOTIF *sweater*

finished sizes

S (M, L, XL) fits 38 (40 1/2, 43, 45 1/2)" (96.5 [103, 109, 115.5] cm) bust circumference.

21 (22 1/4, 23 1/2, 24 3/4)" (53.5 [56.5, 59.5, 63] cm) long.

Sweater shown is size S.

yarn

Fingering weight (#1 Super Fine) in black/ brown/olive, red multi, red/coral, red/ black, and red rainbow.

SHOWN: Koigu Premium Painter's Palette Merino (KPPM) (100% merino wool; 175 yd [160 m]/1.75 oz [50 g]): #P315 (MC [black/ brown/olive], 5 skeins; #P621 (A [red multi]); #P632 (B [red/coral]); #P604 (C [red/black]); #P912 (D [red rainbow]), 1 skein each.

hook

D/3 (3.25 mm) or size needed to obtain gauge.

notions

Tapestry needle.

gauge

Each motif measures 1 1/4" (3.2 cm) in diameter.

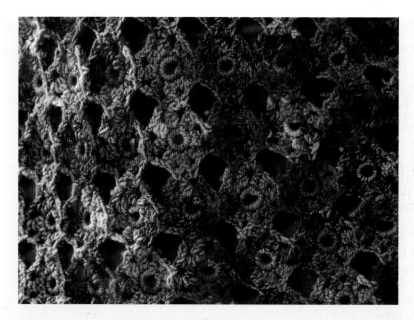

This is a more challenging project for those of you who are ready for something a little more complex. It is constructed of many tiny circles, joined together as it's worked. I am crazy about red and so I find the mixing of a few shades of red against a dark neutral background very exciting. The varying reds make the starburst design shimmer. A deep purple background with the starburst in shades of silvery blue would be lovely as well.

notes

» Beginning chain does not count as a stitch.

» Sweater is worked from side to side in one piece, with no seams, joining motifs as they are made. Motifs are joined at two chain spaces for each side.

» Crochet over ends (p. 111) and secure tails diagonally (p. 112) as you work to shorten finishing time.

CONSTRUCTION DIAGRAMS

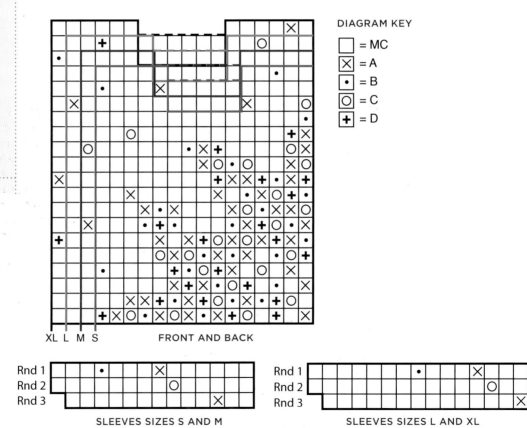

DIAGRAM KEY

☐ = MC
☒ = A
• = B
◉ = C
✛ = D

XL L M S   FRONT AND BACK

Rnd 1
Rnd 2
Rnd 3

SLEEVES SIZES S AND M

Rnd 1
Rnd 2
Rnd 3

SLEEVES SIZES L AND XL

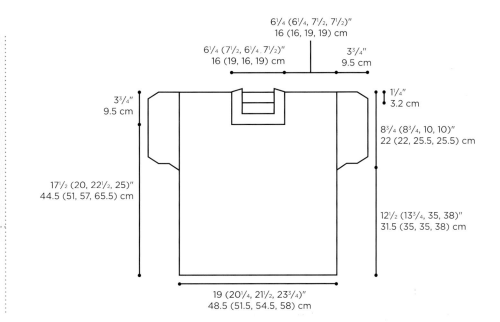

6¼ (6¼, 7½, 7½)"
16 (16, 19, 19) cm

6¼ (7½, 6¼, 7½)"
16 (19, 16, 19) cm

3¾"
9.5 cm

3¾"
9.5 cm

1¼"
3.2 cm

8¾ (8¾, 10, 10)"
22 (22, 25.5, 25.5) cm

17½ (20, 22½, 25)"
44.5 (51, 57, 65.5) cm

12½ (13¾, 35, 38)"
31.5 (35, 35, 38) cm

19 (20¼, 21½, 23¾)"
48.5 (51.5, 54.5, 58) cm

sweater

Follow the construction diagram at left for placement of colors.

FIRST MOTIF

With MC, ch 5, sl st in first ch to form ring.

RND 1: Ch 1, 8 sc into ring, join with sl st in first sc.

RND 2: Ch 3, dc in same sc, ch 3, [dc2tog in next sc, ch 3] 7 times, sl st in first dc to join. Fasten off.

SECOND AND REMAINING MOTIFS

See stitch diagram A on p. 108 for assistance.

Work Rnd 1 as for First Motif.

RND 2: Ch 3, dc in same sc, ch 1, sl st to corresponding ch-3 sp of adjoining motif, ch 1, dc2tog in next sc, ch 1, sl st to next ch-3 sp of same adjoining motif, ch 1, (dc2tog in next sc, ch 3) around, joining to other motifs on one or more sides in the same manner as needed. Fasten off.

Make and join 490 (552, 626, 696) motifs following the construction diagram at left. Work in rows from bottom to shoulder, beginning at right back and working across to left back. Continuing around to front, work left front, leaving 7 (7, 8, 8) motifs unjoined at upper edge for sleeve opening. Join top motifs of front shoulders to top motifs of back shoulders as you go. Continue across to right front. For final row of front, join right front motifs to first row of back motifs, leaving 7 (7, 8, 8) motifs unjoined at upper edge for sleeve opening.

FIRST SLEEVE

See sleeves construction diagram (S and M or L and XL) on p. 106 for assistance.

RND 1: Beginning at underarm of body make and join upper right motif of Sleeve construction diagram. Make and join motifs for first round of sleeve, joining each to armhole of body and to each other—14 (14, 16, 16) motifs. Join last motif to first motif of rnd, leaving a gap at the underarm with six "sides."

RND 2: Make and join motifs for 2nd rnd of sleeve.

RND 3 (DEC RND): First motif: Work Rnd 1 as for First Motif.

RND 2: Ch 3, dc in same sc, ch 1, sl st in next two ch-3 sps of adjoining motif, ch 1, dc2tog in next sc of working motif, ch 1, sl st in next two ch-3 sps of next adjoining motif, ch 1, finish as for Rnd 2 of First Motif. Make and join rem motifs as for first rnd of sleeve, joining last motif to first motif—13 (13, 15, 15) motifs.

GUSSET

See stitch diagram B at right for assistance.

Fill the six-sided gap at the underarm with a gusset motif:

Ch 4, sl st in first ch to form ring.

RND 1: Ch 1, 6 sc into ring, sl st in first sc to join.

RND 2: Ch 3, dc in first sc, ch 1, sl st to joined ch-sp of 1 motif, bordering gap, ch 1, [dc2tog in next sc, ch 1, sl st to joined ch-sp of next motif, bordering gap, ch 1] 5 times. Sl st in top of ch-3. Fasten off.

Make 2nd sleeve as for First Sleeve.

FINISHING

With A, make and join 1 round of motifs to fill in neckline.

Gently steam block (p. 118) sweater to finished measurements.

DIAGRAM A

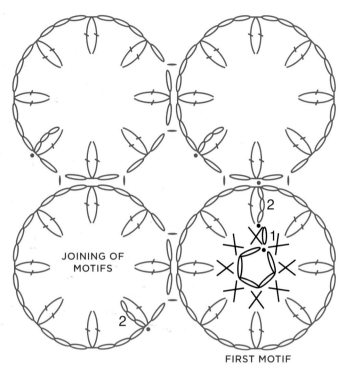

JOINING OF MOTIFS

FIRST MOTIF

DIAGRAM B

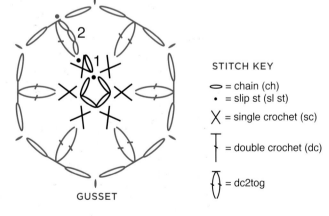

GUSSET

STITCH KEY

⌒ = chain (ch)

• = slip st (sl st)

X = single crochet (sc)

┬ = double crochet (dc)

= dc2tog

COLORWORK *techniques*

There are a few techniques that will make colorwork infinitely more approachable and fun to do. Once you master these few simple techniques you will be well equipped to crochet with color fearlessly!

CHANGING COLORS

Obviously, using lots of colors means changing colors often. When you change colors in crochet, the final loop of the crochet stitch shows up as part of the next stitch. You can see this when you come to a stitch where a color change occurs.

ADD A NEW COLOR

This example is given in single crochet. (Adjust stitch as necessary, but always add the new color as the last loop drawn through all loops on hook.)

Insert hook into a stitch, yarn over hook and draw up a loop (figure 1). Holding the new color yarn behind the work, drop the old color yarn and loop the new color yarn over the hook (figure 2); draw it through both loops on hook (figure 3). Continue with the new color yarn.

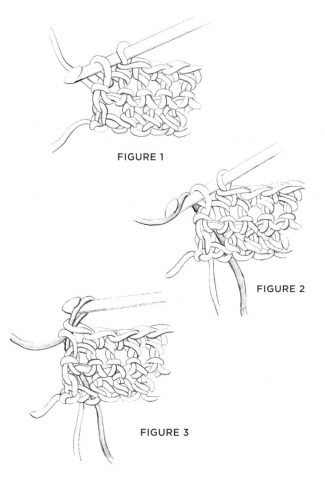

FIGURE 1

FIGURE 2

FIGURE 3

WORKING IN TAILS

Lots of color means lots of yarn tails to deal with. There are several options for working in tails.

CROCHET OVER ENDS

Crocheting over ends is easily done as you work and is well suited for tighter fabrics with shorter stitches (such as single or half double crochet).

Once the color change is made (see Changing Colors left), cut the old color yarn leaving a tail several inches long. Hold both the old color and the new color tails together across the top of the stitches of the previous row (figure 1). Crochet the next several stitches around both tails by inserting the hook into the next stitch under the tails and pulling up a loop, then completing the stitch over the tails, enclosing them inside the stitches (figure 2). Continue crocheting around the tails until they are completely covered (figure 3).

FIGURE 1

FIGURE 2

FIGURE 3

TIPS

» Give the tails a little tug as you crochet so that they are visible beyond the stitches; after several stitches, gently stretch the piece back out so that the tails retreat back into the fabric and disappear.

» Fabrics worked in slip stitch, single, or half double crochet hide tails well.

SECURE TAILS DIAGONALLY

Taller stitches (such as double and treble crochet) and lacy motifs don't hide ends as well as denser fabrics do, so securing tails diagonally along the back of the piece works better than trying to crochet over them.

Using a hook a size or two smaller than the one you are crocheting with, pull the tails through a few inches of loops on the back of the work. Work the tails through loops in a diagonal rather than a straight line and avoid working over gaps so that the tails won't show through on the right side of the fabric. Once the tails are secured, give the piece a gentle tug to loosen it, causing the ends of the tails to recede into the fabric.

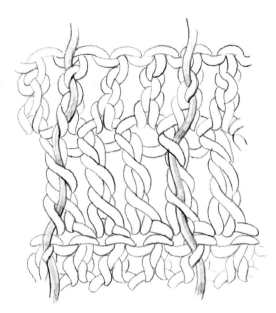

TIPS

» If you are making something with a back side that won't show, such as the Triangles Tuffet on p. 87, you can simply tie the ends together to secure them, then pull them through to the back of the work.

STRANDING

Stranded crochet involves following a graph to create picture or tapestry crochet. Carrying the colors across the back of the work allows you to avoid creating a large number of tails. I find that working stranded crochet in the round is especially enjoyable because you are always looking at the front of the stitches, as there is no turning at the end of a row (see the Clover Hat on p. 79 and the Swirls Pillow on p. 83).

Drop the old color at the final step of the last stitch of that section, finishing the stitch with the new color (see Changing Colors on p. 110). Continue with the new color, carrying the old color across the back of the piece (figure 1, viewed from the back). Every few stitches, crochet over the carried yarn by holding it behind the next stitch and inserting the hook into the stitch and under the carried yarn (figure 2), then complete the stitch as usual. This will keep the strands from becoming too long and catching on fingers and buttons. Continue carrying and securing the old yarn along the back in this manner (figure 3, viewed from the back).

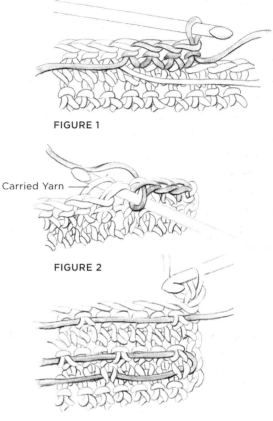

FIGURE 1

Carried Yarn

FIGURE 2

FIGURE 3

WORKING IN THE ROUND

For working in the round, I use one of two methods, spiral or closed.

SPIRAL

The spiral is created by continuously working around in a spiral without joining rows, allowing each round to flow into the next. This method is best for single color projects, where an uneven line at the end of each round won't be noticeable.

CLOSED

The closed method is created by joining the last stitch of each round to the beginning stitch of the round with a slip stitch (count the chains at the beginning of the round as a stitch). This makes each round finished and separate from the previous round, leaving a nearly invisible jog or "seam." This method is better for designs requiring precise pattern definition where all the stitches and rounds need to line up in order to avoid an obvious break. When using the closed method, it's a good idea to mark the beginning of the round with a split-ring marker in the first stitch.

FINISHING *techniques*

Here are a few finishing techniques that will help you with the details that complete your crochet projects.

BORDERS AND BANDS

Crochet stitches are not square, so when making button or buttonhole bands, trims, borders, and collars you can't just work one stitch for every row or you may end up with a border that doesn't fit properly. One of the many beautiful things about crochet is that if your band or collar looks too tight or too ruffled, you can give it a tug to take it out and start again. However, it helps to have a plan to ensure that your border or band turns out correctly. I have found the following formulas to be pretty reliable.

SINGLE CROCHET (SC) FABRIC

Work the border/band as follows. *1 sc into each of the next 3 rows, skip 1 row and rep from *.

HALF DOUBLE CROCHET (HDC) FABRIC

Work the border/band as follows. *2 hdc into each of the next 3 rows, 1 hdc into the following row and rep from *.

DOUBLE CROCHET (DC) FABRIC

Work the border/band as follows. *3 dc into each of the next 2 rows, 2 dc into the following row and rep from *.

I tend to avoid complicated edging patterns, largely because lengthy stitch pattern repeats or very tall stitches can make working the border onto the finished piece very complicated. I stick to stitch patterns with repeats of four stitches or fewer, using shorter stitches. If you become totally enamored with a pretty lacy stitch pattern with a long repeat, make the border separately, using a multiple of stitches that gets closest to the length of your piece and sew it on when it's finished.

SEAMS

Seaming can be done in several ways. The following stitches are what I use most often to create secure seams.

HERRINGBONE STITCH

Herringbone stitch works well for seaming two pieces that line up stitch by stitch (see the Swirls Pillow on p. 83 and the Pleated Hat on p. 13).

With right sides facing, lay the edges of the two pieces side by side. Using a threaded tapestry needle, sew through the first stitch on one piece, taking the needle from the wrong side up through the stitch to the right side. *Sew through the corresponding stitch on the opposite piece, taking the needle from the wrong side up through the stitch to the right side. Repeat from * to the end, stretching the piece gently at intervals as you sew to keep the seam from puckering.

WHIPSTITCH

With right side of work facing and working through edge stitch, bring threaded needle out from back to front along edge of piece. To whipstitch one piece into place on top of another, simply bring the needle through all layers, working through the edge stitches of the piece being stitched on.

MATTRESS STITCH

Mattress stitch works best for seaming pieces that line up row by row, such as the front and back pieces of garments (see the Firefly Cardigan on p. 17 and the Blocks Coat on p. 57).

With right sides facing, lay the edges of the two pieces side by side. Using a threaded tapestry needle, pick up two bars of the first stitch on one piece (figure 1). *Keeping the yarn loose, take the needle to the front of the opposite piece and pick up two bars of the corresponding stitch (figure 2). Repeat from * (figure 3) to the end, pulling the yarn to tighten the seam every few stitches. Be careful not to pull so tightly that the seam becomes puckered.

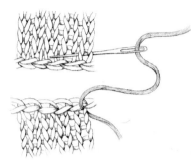

FIGURE 1

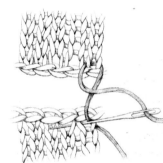

FIGURE 2

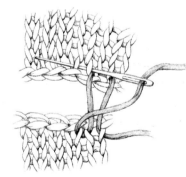

FIGURE 3

BLOCKING

I find that most things I make don't require strenuous blocking, and often a good steaming works very well. However, it's important to know about blocking techniques and when to use them.

STEAM BLOCKING

Steaming with a good iron works very well to smooth and set the shape of most fibers. It isn't necessary to press down on the fabric, simply set your iron to the steam setting, then let it hover over the piece and press the steam button a few times. Move the piece and repeat until you have a nice smooth surface. For fitted garments and pieces that need to be sewn together, pin the piece to the finished measurements and shape required after steaming, then leave the piece to dry.

WET BLOCKING

Wet blocking works well for lace and pieces with open motifs like the Grenada Shawl on page 29. To wet block, simply dampen the piece with a spray bottle and then gently stretch and pin the piece to the finished measurements and the required shape, then leave the piece to dry.

ABBREVIATIONS

blo	back loop(s) only
CC	contrasting color
ch	chain
ch-	refers to chain or space previously made
ch-sp	chain space
cm	centimeter(s)
cont	continue
dc	double crochet
dec	decrease(s)
dtr	double treble crochet
foll	follow/follows/following
g	gram(s)
hdc	half double crochet
hdc2tog	half double crochet 2 together
inc	increase(s)
MC	main color
m	meter(s)
mm	millimeter(s)
oz	ounce(s)
patt	pattern
pm	place marker
prev	previous
rem	remaining
rep	repeat
rnd	round
sc	single crochet
sc2tog	single crochet 2 together
sl st	slip stitch
sp(s)	space(s)
st(s)	stitch(es)
tch	turning chain
tog	together
tr	treble crochet
tr2tog	treble crochet 2 together
v-st	v stitch
yd	yard(s)
yo	yarnover
*	repeat instructions following asterisk as directed
**	repeat instructions between asterisks as directed
()	alternate measurements or instructions
[]	work bracketed instructions specified number of times

TERMS

Facing: The term facing is used to indicate when something should be facing up. For example, "with right side facing" means that the right side of the fabric should be facing up.

Right Side: The right side of a crocheted fabric is the front, or the side that should appear on the outside of a garment.

Wrong Side: The wrong side of a crocheted fabric is the back, or the side that should appear on the inside of a garment.

GLOSSARY

SQUARE KNOT

Begin with 2 yarns, make an overhand knot (see figure 1 for an example of an overhand knot) by passing the right end over the left end. Make another overhand knot with the tails of the two yarns, this time passing the left end over the right end (figure 2). Pull tight.

FIGURE 1

FIGURE 2

CROCHET CHAIN (CH)

Make a slipknot and place it on crochet hook. *Yarn over hook and draw through loop on hook. Repeat from * for the desired number of stitches.

SINGLE CROCHET (SC)

Insert hook into a stitch, yarn over hook and draw up a loop (figure 1), yarn over hook and draw it through both loops on hook (figure 2).

FIGURE 1   **FIGURE 2**

SLIP STITCH (SL ST)

*Insert hook into stitch, yarn over hook and draw loop through stitch and loop on hook. Repeat from *.

ADJUSTABLE RING

Wrap yarn around your index finger 3 times (figure 1). Slide the loop just made off your index finger (figure 2) and chain 1 into the loop (figure 3)—adjustable ring made.

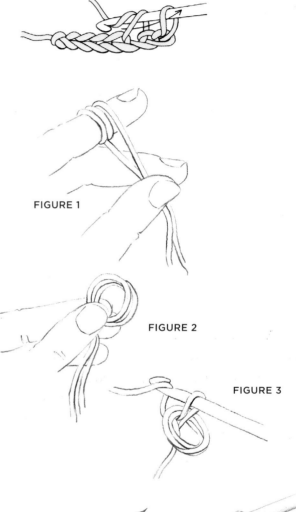

FIGURE 1

FIGURE 2

FIGURE 3

HALF DOUBLE CROCHET (HDC)

*Yarn over hook, insert hook into a stitch, yarn over hook and draw up a loop (3 loops on hook), yarn over hook (figure 1) and draw it through all loops on hook (figure 2). Repeat from *.

FIGURE 1   FIGURE 2

HALF DOUBLE CROCHET 2 TOGETHER (HDC2TOG)

Yarn over hook, insert hook into next indicated stitch, yarn over hook and draw up a loop, yarn over hook (3 loops on hook; figure 1), insert hook into next indicated stitch, yarn over hook and draw up a loop (5 loops on hook; figure 2), yarn over hook and draw it through all loops on hook (figure 3)—1 stitch decreased.

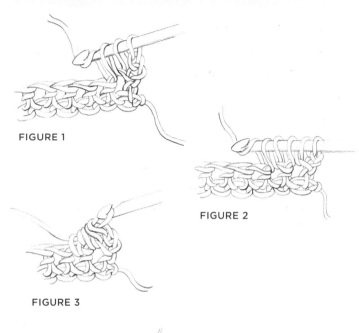

FIGURE 1

FIGURE 2

FIGURE 3

DOUBLE CROCHET (DC)

*Yarn over hook, insert hook into a stitch, yarn over hook and draw up a loop (3 loops on hook; figure 1), yarn over hook and draw it through 2 loops (figure 2), yarn over hook and draw it through remaining 2 loops on hook (figure 3). Repeat from *

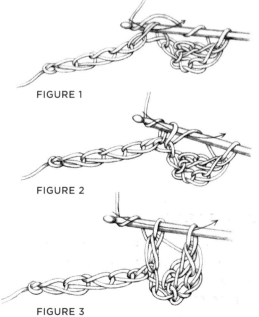

FIGURE 1

FIGURE 2

FIGURE 3

DOUBLE CROCHET 2 TOGETHER (DC2TOG)

Yarn over hook, insert hook into next indicated stitch, yarn over hook and draw up a loop (figure 1), yarn over hook and draw yarn through 2 loops, yarn over hook, insert hook into next indicated stitch and draw up a loop (4 loops on hook), yarn over hook, draw yarn through 2 loops (figure 2), yarn over hook and draw yarn through remaining 3 loops on hook (figure 3). Completed dc2tog—1 stitch decreased (figure 4).

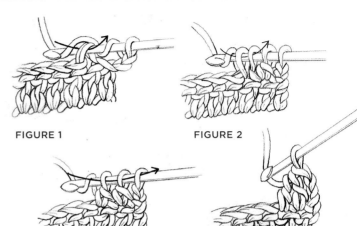

FIGURE 1   FIGURE 2

FIGURE 3   FIGURE 4

TREBLE CROCHET (TR)

*Wrap yarn around hook twice, insert hook into next indicated stitch, yarn over hook and draw up a loop (4 loops on hook; figure 1), yarn over hook and draw it through 2 loops (figure 2), yarn over hook and draw it through the next 2 loops (figure 3), yarn over hook and draw it through remaining 2 loops on hook as before. Repeat from *.

DOUBLE TREBLE CROCHET (DTR)

*Wrap yarn around hook 3 times, insert hook into stitch, yarn over hook and draw up a loop (5 loops on hook), [yarn over hook and draw it through 2 loops] 4 times. Repeat from *.

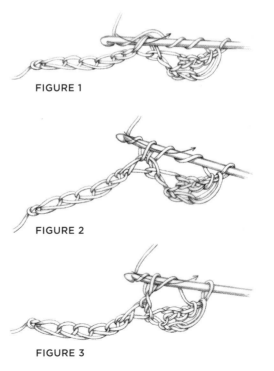

FIGURE 1

FIGURE 2

FIGURE 3

TREBLE CROCHET 2 TOGETHER (TR2TOG)

*Wrap yarn around hook twice, insert hook into next indicated stitch, yarn over hook and draw up a loop (4 loops on hook), [yarn over hook, draw through 2 loops] twice (figure 1). Wrap yarn around hook twice, insert hook into next indicated stitch, yarn over hook and draw up a loop (5 loops on hook), [yarn over hook, draw through 2 loops] twice (3 loops on hook; figure 2), yarn over hook and draw through all loops on hook (figure 3)—1 stitch decreased.

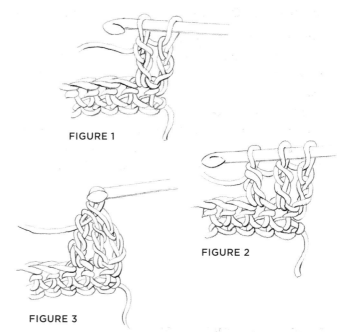

FIGURE 1

FIGURE 2

FIGURE 3

RESOURCES

CASCADE YARNS

cascadeyarns.com
Cascade 220 Wool
Luna

CRYSTAL PALACE YARNS

straw.com
160 23rd St.
Richmond, CA 94804
Deco Ribbon
Panda Silk

DMC CREATIVE WORLD

dmc-usa.com
77 South Hackensack Ave.,
Bldg. 10F
South Kearny, NJ 07032-4688
(973) 589-0606
Perle Cotton #5

KOIGU WOOL DESIGNS

koigu.com
PO Box 158
Chatsworth, ON N0H1G0
Canada
(888) 765-9665
Koigu Painter's Palette Premium
Merino (KPPM)

LORNA'S LACES

lornaslaces.net
4229 N. Honore St.
Chicago, IL 60613
(773) 935-3803
Helen's Lace

MALABRIGO YARN

malabrigoyarn.com
(786) 866-6187
Merino worsted

MISSION FALLS

missionfalls.com
5333 Casgrain #1204
Montreal, QC
H2T 1X3
(877) 244-1204
1824 Wool

NORO/ KFI

knittingfever.com
PO Box 336
315 Bayview Ave.
Amityville, NY 11701
(516) 546-3600
Silk Garden by Noro

WESTMINSTER FIBERS

westminsterfibers.com
165 Ledge St.
Nashua, NH 03060
(800) 445-9276
Rowan Kidsilk Haze
Rowan 4-Ply Soft

SHEEP SHOP YARN COMPANY

sheepshopyarn.com
PO Box 1444
East Greenwich, RI 02818
(401) 398-7656
Sheep Shop Three

SKACEL

skacelknitting.com
info@skacelknitting.com
(800) 255-1278
Zitron Trekking XXL

THE FIBRE COMPANY/ KELBOURNE WOOLENS

thefibreco.com
915 N. 28th St. 2nd Fl.
Philadelphia, PA 19130
(215) 687-5534
Terra

INDEX

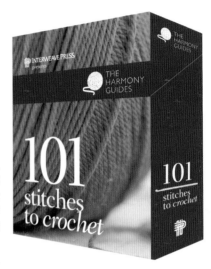